CRYPTIC MASONRY.

A

MANUAL OF THE COUNCIL;

OR,

MONITORIAL INSTRUCTIONS

IN THE DEGREES OF

ROYAL AND SELECT MASTER.

WITH AN

ADDITIONAL SECTION

ON THE

SUPER-EXCELLENT MASTER'S DEGREE.

BY

ALBERT G. MACKEY, M. D.,

AUTHOR OF A "LEXICON OF FREEMASONRY," "MANUAL OF THE LODGE,"
"BOOK OF THE CHAPTER," "THE RITUALIST," ETC., ETC.

———————

NEW YORK:

MAYNARD, MERRILL, & CO.,

29, 31, AND 33 EAST NINETEENTH STREET.

1897.

TO

BROTHER DAVID CLARKE,

OF HARTFORD,

PAST GRAND MASTER OF THE GRAND LODGE OF CONNECTICUT.

MY DEAR BROTHER CLARKE,

A friendship which began fourteen years ago, at Lexington, in Kentucky, has not been diminished by the attrition of time, or weakened by the distance of our respective dwelling-places. I therefore inscribe this little book with your name, as a slight memorial of the kindly feelings that exist between yourself and

THE AUTHOR.

CONTENTS.

PREFACE.

FOR a long time past I have been approached by several of my Masonic friends with a suggestion that, as I had already compiled a "Manual of the Lodge" and a "Book of the Chapter," I should complete the series of monitorial works by adding one on the Degrees of the Council of Royal and Select Masters. In endeavoring to comply, to the best of my abilities, with this request, I have sought to follow the same plan which was pursued by me in the compilation of my other Monitors, and to make my book something more than a mere collection of Scriptural passages and charges to candidates. The Masonic student who is desirous of pursuing his researches into these higher arcana of the institution will therefore, I think, find in these pages some information on points of Masonic science and history, a knowledge of which is essentially necessary to a thorough comprehension of the moral design and symbolism of the degrees upon whose study he has entered. This, at least, has been the end that I endeavored to attain. How far I have succeeded, or in how much I have failed, is not for me to determine.

The American Rite, the name now very generally conceded to that series of degrees which are conferred in this country, is a modification of the English or Ancient York Rite, and consists, by the universal consent of all Masonic ritualists for more than half a century, of nine degrees, commencing with the Entered Apprentice, and terminating with the Select Master. To this series I desire to confine the Rite, and have no wish, as I have no authority, to extend it beyond the original number.

The degree of Super-Excellent Master I therefore reject from the Rite, not because it is the recent invention of some prolific brain, for it is, at least, as old as some of the acknowledged degrees of the Rite —such, for instance, as that of Most Excellent Master—but because neither Webb, nor Cole, nor Cross, nor any other more recent Masonic ritualist, has recognized it as constituting any part of the Rite. It has, on the contrary, until very recently, been always conferred as an honorary or detached degree, and as such it should be considered.

But as the degree is in itself interesting, and supplies, in its ceremonies and legend, a desirable commentary on, and exemplification of, an important portion of the Royal Arch; and as, within a few years, many Councils in the Northern and Western

States have admitted it into the series of degrees which they confer, I have, as a matter of convenience to them, inserted in the present work the necessary monitorial instructions, without any desire or intention to see it elevated into a regular degree. which I trust it will never be, because its introduction as such would impair the symmetry of the Rite, which, as now constituted, presents an exact circle of Masonic science, and which, from the Apprentice's degree to the Select Master's, begins and ends in the search for the TRUE WORD, with which the Super-Excellent alone, of all the degrees, has nothing to do.

The difficulties with which I have had to contend in the compilation of this work have been of no trifling magnitude. No separate Monitor of the Council degrees has ever before been published, and from none of the works of Masonic ritualists, who have incidentally treated of these degrees, have I been able to obtain much assistance. The earlier and original editions of Webb contain no reference to the Royal and Select degrees. Cole, who was the first to pay any attention to them, gives but one page to the Royal Master, and that consists altogether of citations from the Bible, and three and a half to the Select Master, of which three consist entirely of Scriptural extracts. Cross, who first placed them in their regular order in the Rite, embraces all that he has to say of both degrees in five pages of his

"Chart," and these consist principally of passages of Scripture, most of them being wholly inapplicable to the design and character of the degrees. Notwithstanding this, all his successors—who have constructed their Monitors on the model of their prototype, with a rigid exactitude that would be worthy of a Chinese tailor, who copies the very rents in the pattern of the vestment that he is making—have, with wonderful unanimity, copied these useless and inappropriate citations from Scripture. Finding no use nor application for them in the ceremonies or the traditions of the degrees, I have omitted them.

To give a single instance of the inaccuracy of the authorities from which alone I could receive any guidance, let me refer to that particular plate under the head of "Royal Master" in Cross's "Chart," in which he exhibits Adoniram and the Builder of the Temple engaged in conversation within the Sanctum Sanctorum, which is represented as completely finished, and the Ark of the Covenant in its proper place. Now, when this conversation took place, as referred to in the legend of the Royal degree, the Holy of Holies had not been completed nor consecrated, nor had the Ark, so ostentatiously exhibited in the plate of Cross, as yet any place in the temple. The anachronism is as great as if a modern painter were to depict the "Pilgrim Fathers," after they had landed from the Mayflower, as assembled for consultation within the walls of Faneuil Hall. Such errors are calculated to mislead the Masonic student in questions of history, and I have sedulously avoided them.

In the "Manual" compiled some years ago by Bro. Robert Macoy, there is, as to the ritual, no additions to those of Cross, but the author has added a form of installation for the officers of a subordinate Council, from which I have derived some advantage. The forms for the installation of Grand Officers and for the consecration of new Councils are entirely my own.

In the absence of every thing except the most meager details, I was compelled to have recourse to my own researches, to depend upon my own judgment, and to exercise some independence of thought. I have consequently furnished a work of which, whatever may be the character of the execution, nineteen-twentieths at least are original. There is, however, nothing in it that the most rigid critic can construe into an innovation on the landmarks. The edifice of Cryptic Masonry is unaltered. I have only opened and exposed to the view of those to whom it is lawful to behold, those interior apartments which no Masonic writer has hitherto explored.

I take great pleasure in acknowledging my indebt edness to Companion Brig.-Gen. Geo. W. Balloch, and to Companion Thomas Snow, of New Hampshire, through whose united kindness I have been put in possession of much valuable information, especially in reference to the present working of the Super-Excellent degree in those Councils which have adopted it.

A word in reference to the title *Cryptic Masonry.* The epithet "Cryptic" was first used, I think, by Bro. Rob. Morris, to designate the Council degrees. It is derived from the Latin *crypticus*, which means *subterranean* or *concealed*, and that from the Greek *kruptē*, which signifies a *vault* or *subterranean passage.* The caves, or cells under ground, in which the primitive Christians celebrated their secret worship, were called *cryptæ*, and the vaults beneath our modern churches receive the name of crypts. The expression, "Cryptic Masonry," therefore substantially denotes "Masonry of the Secret Vault." Hence, as it is a most appropriate term when applied to the Royal and Select degrees, I have not hesitated to adopt it.

EIGHTH DEGREE.

ROYAL MASTER.

SYMBOLICAL DESIGN.

THE ceremonies of the degree of Royal Master are very brief and simple—briefer and simpler, indeed, than those of any of the preceding degrees. Symbolically, however, they present one great idea—the truly masonic one—of the laborer seeking for his reward. Throughout all the symbolism of masonry, from the first to the last degree, the search for the WORD has been considered but as a symbolic expression for the search after Truth. The attainment of this Truth has always been acknowledged to be the great object and design of all Masonic labor. Divine Truth—the knowledge of God—concealed in the old Cabalistic doctrine, under the symbol of his Ineffable Name, and typified in the masonic system, under the mystical expression of the True Word, is the reward proposed to every mason who has faithfully wrought his task. It is, in short, the " Master's wages."

Now all this is beautifully symbolized in the degree of Royal Master. The reward had been promised, and the time had now come, as Adoniram thought, when the promise was to be redeemed and the true word—divine Truth—was to be imparted. Hence, in the person of Adoniram, or the Royal Master, we see symbolized the speculative mason, who, having labored to complete his spiritual temple, comes to the Divine Master that he may receive his reward, and that his labor may be consummated by the acquisition of Truth. But the temple that he has been building is the temple of this life; that first temple which must be destroyed by death, that the second temple of the future life may be built on its foundations. And in this first temple the truth cannot be found. We must be content with its substitute.

This, then, is the symbolism of the Royal Master's degree.

HISTORICAL SUMMARY.

The events recorded in the degree of Royal Master, looking at them in a legendary point of view, must have occurred at the building of the first temple, and during that brief period of time after the death of the Builder which is embraced between the discovery of his body and its "masonic interment." In all the initiations into the mysteries of the ancient world, there was, as it is well known to scholars, a legend of the violent death of some distinguished personage, to whose memory the particular mystery was consecrated; of the concealment of the body and of its subsequent discovery. That part of the initiation which referred to the concealment of the body was called the *aphanism*, from a Greek verb which signifies "to conceal," and that part which referred to the subsequent finding was called the "*euresis*," from another Greek verb, which signifies "to discover." It is impossible to avoid seeing the coincidences between this system of initiation and that practiced in the masonry of the third degree.

But the ancient initiation was not terminated by the euresis or discovery. Up to that point the cere-monies had been funereal and lugubrious in their character. But now they were changed from wailing to rejoicing. Other ceremonies were performed by which the restoration of the personage to life or his apotheosis or change to immortality was represented, and then came the *autopsy* or illumination of the neophyte, when he was invested with a full knowledge of all the religious doctrines which it was the object and design of the ancient mysteries to teach, —when, in a word, he was instructed in Divine Truth.

Now a similar course is pursued in masonry. Here also there is an illumination, a symbolical teaching, or, as we call it, an *investiture* with that which is the representative of Divine Truth. The communication to the candidate in the Master's degree of that which is admitted to be merely a representation of or a substitution for that symbol of Divine Truth, the search for which, under the name of the *true word*, makes so important a part of the degree, however imperfect it may be, in comparison with that more thorough knowledge which only future researches can enable the Master Mason to attain, constitutes the *autopsy* of the third degree. Now the principal event recorded in the degree of Royal Master, the interview between Adoniram and his two Royal Masters, is to be placed precisely at that juncture of time which is between the euresis, or discovery, in the Master Mason's degree, and the autopsy, or investiture with the great secret. It occurred between the discovery by means of the sprig of acacia, and the final interment. It was at the time when Solomon and his colleague, Hiram of Tyre, were in profound consultation as to the mode of repairing the loss which they then supposed had befallen them.

We must come to this conclusion, because there is abundant reference, both in the organized form of the Council and in the ritual of the degree, to the death as an event that had already occurred ; and, on the other hand, while it is evident that Solomon had been made acquainted with the failure to recover, on the person of the Builder, that which had been lost, there is no reference whatever to the well-known *substitution* which was made at the time of the interment.

If, therefore, as is admitted by all masonic ritualists, the *substitution* was precedent and preliminary to the establishment of the Master Mason's degree, it is evident that at the time when the degree of Royal Master is said to have been founded in the ancient temple by our "first Most Excellent Grand Master," all persons present, except the first and second officers, must have been merely Fellow-Craft Masons. In compliance with this tradition, therefore, a Royal Master is at this day supposed to represent a Fellow-Craft in the search of, and making his demand for, that reward which was to elevate him to the rank of a Master Mason.

OPENING OF THE COUNCIL.

A Council of Royal Masters consists of the following eight officers :—

THRICE ILLUSTRIOUS GRAND MASTER.
ILLUSTRIOUS HIRAM OF TYRE.
PRINCIPAL CONDUCTOR OF THE WORKS.
MASTER OF THE EXCHEQUER.
MASTER OF FINANCES.
CAPTAIN OF THE GUARDS.
CONDUCTOR OF THE COUNCIL.
STEWARD.

Of these the first three represent, respectively, Solomon, king of Israel ; Hiram, king of Tyre ; and Adoniram, the Chief of the Fellow-Crafts, who, after the death of the Builder, was promoted to the position of Principal Conductor of the Works.

The Thrice Illustrious Grand Master is seated on the throne in the East (1) ; the Illustrious Hiram of Tyre is on his right (2), seated at a triangular table, a similar table on the left being unoccupied. The Principal Conductor of the Works is in the West (3) ; the Master of the Exchequer in the South (4) ;

the Master of Finances in the North (5); the
Captain of the Guards in front and to the right of
the throne (6); the Conductor of the Council on the
right of the Principal Conductor of the 'Works (7);
and the Steward, who acts as Tiler in the usual
place of that officer (8). The following diagram
will explain these positions :—

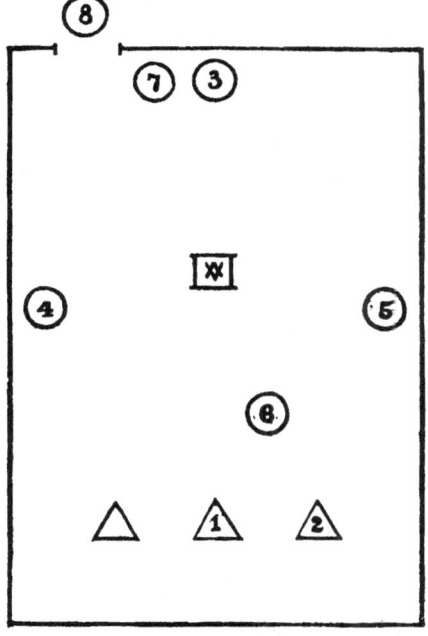

The symbolic colors of a Royal Master are black
and red. The black is significant of the grief of

the Craft for the loss of their Operative Grand Master, and the red, of his blood, which was shed in defense of his integrity. Hence the apron and collar of a Royal Master should be black, lined and edged with red. The apron must be triangular in form, in allusion to the sacred Delta.

The place of meeting is called the "Council Chamber," and represents the private apartment of the King of Israel, in which he is said to have met his two colleagues during the erection of the temple, for the purpose of consultation on all matters relating to the craft.

When a candidate is initiated, he is said to be "honored with the degree of Royal Master."

PRAYER.*

ON OPENING A COUNCIL OF ROYAL MASTERS.

Almighty God, thou art from everlasting to everlasting; unchangeable in thy being; unbounded and incomprehensible. Thou didst

* This prayer, and the one for closing, were in use by the Supreme Council of Sovereign Grand Inspectors General, from the first introduction of the degree into this country by that body. The ritual in my possession, which contains these prayers, was copied by the Grand Commander, about the year 1822, from the authorized ritual in the archives. Their beauty and antiquity justify their retention in every manual of Cryptic Masonry.

speak into being this vast fabric of the Universe. We adore and bow before thee with reverential awe, and acknowledge our sins and misdeeds, for thou hast promised to heal our backslidings and to love us freely. Look down from thy holy habitation and bless us with thy approbation. Teach us to praise thy holy Name aright, for thou art the God whom we fear, and to whom we bow with humble submission. Lord, hear our prayer, and accept our sacrifice of thanksgiving. *So mote it be. Amen.*

RECEPTION.

The following passages of Scripture are appropriate to the reception of the candidate in this degree:

1 Kings vi. 27.

And he set the cherubim within the inner house; and they stretched forth the wings of the cherubim, so that the wing of the one touched the one wall, and the wing of the other cherub touched the other wall; and their wings touched one another in the midst of the house.

Revelation xxii. 12–14.

And, behold, I come quickly; and my reward is with me, to give every man according as his work shall be. I am Alpha and Omega, the beginning and the end, the first and the last. Blessed are they that do his commandments, that they may have right to the tree of life, and may enter in through the gates into the city.

THE EXTENDED WINGS OF THE CHERUBIM.

The Cherubim were certain figures conspicuous in the ceremonial of the Jewish tabernacle and temple. There is much diversity of opinion among the learned as to their form, but all agree in this : that they were furnished with wings, and that their wings were extended. Two of them were placed in the tabernacle of Moses, in a stooping attitude, at each end of the mercy-seat or covering of the ark, which they overshadowed with their expanded wings. They were afterwards transferred, with the Ark of the Covenant, of which indeed they formed a component part, to the Holy of Holies of King Solomon's Temple. In the intervening space, above the ark and beneath the extended wings, were the Schechinah or sacred flame, that symbolized the Divine Presence, and the letters of the ineffable name of Jehovah. From this is derived that peculiar phrase-

ology of the sacred writers, who always speak of the
Deity as dwelling between the Cherubim ; and when-
ever the Almighty is described as sitting on a throne,
or riding in a triumphal chariot, the Cherubim constitute an important part of the description.

The Cherubim were eminently and purely symbolical. But although there is great diversity of
opinion as to their exact signification, yet there is a
very general agreement that, under some one mani-
festation or another, they allude to and symbolize the
protecting and overshadowing power of the Deity.
When therefore the initiate is received *beneath the
extended wings of the Cherubim*, we are taught by
this symbolism how appropriate it is, that he who
comes to ask and to seek Truth, symbolized by the
True Word, should begin by placing himself under
the protection of that Divine Power who alone is
Truth, and from whom alone Truth can be obtained.

ALPHA AND OMEGA.

Alpha (Λ) is the first and Omega (Ω) is the last
letter of the Greek alphabet, equivalent to the beginning and the end or the first and the last of
any thing. The Jews used the first and last letters
of their alphabet, Aleph and Tau, to express the
same idea, but St. John, although a Hebrew, used

the Grecian letters in the Apocalypse, because he was writing in the Greek language.

Alpha and Omega are adopted as a symbol of the Deity, and are found repeatedly in mediæval paintings attached to representations of Christ as God. Prudentius, in his 9th hymn, gives expression to this idea :—

"Alpha et Omega cognominatur ipse ; fons et clausula, Omnium quæ sunt, fuerunt, vel post futura sunt."

"Alpha and Omega is He called ; the source and end Of all things which are, which were, or will hereafter be."

The passage from the Apocalypse, which is read during the circumambulation, is therefore exceedingly appropriate in referring, by this symbol, to the eternal nature of God, since that is the great truth for which, under the form of the WORD, the candidate is in search.

THE HOLY OF HOLIES.

Previous monitorial writers on this degree have given long descriptions of the Holy of Holies, and of the Ark of the Covenant which was placed within it. But the truth is (if we are guided by the tradition which the degree itself relates), that at the time that the incidents which it describes occurred, the Holy of Holies had not been finished, and the Ark had not yet been deposited in it. The Holy of Holies was still the resort of workmen who were engaged in its construction, and was, as we learn from the very words of the legend, as related by Adoniram, the place where the Builder prepared his designs ; and the Ark was not deposited until the temple was completed and dedicated, neither of which circumstances had taken place at the time commemorated in the ceremonies and legend of the degree.

With the Ark of the Covenant the degree of Royal Master has no connection.

ADONIRAM.

The first notice that we have in Scripture of Adoniram is in the Second Book of Samuel (xx. 24), where he is referred to by the abbreviated form Adoram, as having been " over the tribute " in the house of David, or, as Gesenius translates it, " prefect over the tribute service, or tribute master," that is to say, in modern phrase, he was the chief receiver of the taxes. Clarke accordingly calls him, " Chancellor of the Exchequer." Seven years afterwards we find him exercising the duties of the same office in the household of King Solomon, for it is said (1 Kings iv. 6), that " Adoniram, the son of Abda, was over the tribute." And lastly we hear of him as still occupying the same station in the household of King Rehoboam, the successor of Solomon. Forty-seven years after his first mention in the Book of Samuel, he is stated (1 Kings xii. 16) to have been stoned to death while in the discharge of his duty, by the people, who were justly indignant at the oppressions of his master. Although commentators have been at a loss to determine whether the tax-receiver under David, under Solomon, and under Rehoboam, was the same person, there seems to be no reason to doubt it, for, as Kitto says, "it appears very unlikely that even two persons of the same name should successively bear the same office, in an age when no example occurs of the father's name being given to his son. We find also that not more than forty-seven years elapsed between the first and last mention of the Adoniram who was 'over the tribute,' and as this, although a long term of service, is not too long for one life, and as the person who held the office in the beginning of Rehoboam's reign, had served in it long enough to make himself odious to the people, it appears on the whole most probable, that one and the same person is intended throughout."* All of this however is merely conjectural. Even if the tax-receiver of Solomon

* Encycloped. Biblical Literature.

was the man who held the same office under Rehoboam, we still have no means of knowing whether
the odium he incurred was to be attributed to the
unpopularity of the office or the oppressive conduct
of the officer. In a Masonic point of view, we can
only consider Adoniram as the incorruptible laborer
in the temple and the diligent searcher after truth.
He is, to the Mason, simply a symbol.

Adoniram occupies an important position in the
Masonic system, but the time of action in which he
appears is confined to the period occupied in the
construction of the temple. The legends and traditions which connect him with that edifice derive
their support from a single passage in the First Book
of Kings (v. 14), where it is said that Solomon made
a levy of thirty thousand workmen from among the
Israelites ; that he sent these in courses of ten thousand a month to labor on Mount Lebanon, and that
he placed Adoniram over these as their superintend-
ent. From this brief statement the Adoniramite
Masons have deduced the theory that Adoniram was
the architect of the temple, while the Hiramites, as-
signing this office to Hiram Abif, still believe that
Adoniram occupied an important post in the construction of that edifice. He has been called " the
first of the Fellow-Crafts ;" is said, in one tradition,
to have been the brother-in-law of Hiram Abif, the
latter having demanded of King Solomon the hand

of Adoniram's sister in marriage, and that the nuptials were honored by the kings of Israel and Tyre with a public celebration; while another tradition, preserved in the Royal Master's degree, informs us that he was the one to whom the three Grand Masters had intended first to communicate that knowledge which they had reserved as a fitting reward to be bestowed upon all meritorious craftsmen at the completion of the temple.

Adoniram is the Masonic symbol of the seeker after truth.

THE TRIPLE TRIANGLE.

The triple triangle is one of the oldest symbols of mystical science. It is perhaps better known as the *Pentalpha*, from the Greek *pente*, "five," and *Alpha*, the first letter of the Greek alphabet, whose form is precisely that of the English letter A. It is so called because its peculiar configuration presents the appearance of that letter in five different positions.

In the school of Pythagoras it was adopted as the symbol of health, and each of the five salient points was represented by one of the five letters of the Greek word *ΥΓΕΙΑ* "health." Hence the Pythagoreans placed it at the beginning of their epistles as a form of salutation. The early Christians referred it to the five wounds of the Saviour, because, when properly inscribed upon the representation of a human body, the five points will respectively extend to and touch the side, the two hands, and the two feet. Among the Druids the figure of the pentalpha was worn on the shoes as a symbol of the Deity, and they esteemed it as a sign of safety. It was drawn on cradles, thresholds, and especially on stable doors, in order to keep away wizards and witches, and has been used even at the present day as a protection against demoniacal powers, and is probably the origin of the well-known superstition of the horseshoe among the lower orders. Thus Aubrey, the antiquary, says that "it is a thing very common to nail horseshoes on the thresholds of doors, which is to hinder the power of witches that enter into the house." The mediæval Freemasons considered it a symbol of deep wisdom, and it is found among the architectural ornaments of most of the ecclesiastical edifices of the middle ages.

It is, in Masonic symbology, sometimes called the "Shield of David," and sometimes the "Seal of

Solomon," and is said to have been inscribed, with the tetragrammaton in the center, upon the celebrated Stone of Foundation.

But as a Masonic symbol it peculiarly claims atten· tion from the fact that it forms the outlines of the *five-pointed star*, which is typical of the bond of brotherly love that unites the whole fraternity, and alludes, therefore, to the *five points of fellowship.* It is in this view that the pentalpha or triple triangle is referred to in the Royal Master's degree, as representing the intimate union that existed between our three Ancient Grand Masters, and which is commemorated by the living pentalpha at the closing of every Royal Arch Chapter.

THE BROKEN SQUARE.

The square, containing four equal sides and four equal angles, is the most perfect figure in geometry. Hence in Masonry it is the universally acknowledged

symbol of perfection. And as that condition of
perfection was so pre-eminently exhibited in the mystical union of our three Grand Masters, whose Wisdom, Strength, and Beauty devised, erected, and
adorned the temple, so the Broken Square, by the
dismemberment of the perfect figure, is emblematic
of that imperfection and loss which ensued upon
the untimely death of one of the three.

If, therefore, the Triple Triangle is peculiarly
appropriate to the Royal Arch, as symbolic of the
perfect union of the Illustrious Three, so is the
Broken Square equally appropriate to the Royal
Master, as symbolic of the unhappy dissolution of
that union by death. The Broken Square is pre-
eminently the symbol of this degree.

CLOSING OF THE COUNCIL.

A Council of Royal Masters is closed with
the following

PRAYER.*

Incomprehensibly holy, supremely good and

---

* This prayer and the benediction, as well as the opening
prayer, are very old and of high authority. See the note on
the prayer at opening, page 20.

All-wise God, thou art our father and our friend; we are thy people and the sheep of thy pasture. Prostrating ourselves before thee, we acknowledge our unworthiness to appear in thy presence. But thou hast said that thou art the Lord God, mercifully forgiving sin and transgression. Pardon, we beseech thee, what thou hast seen amiss in us at this time. Confirm and strengthen us in every good work, and take us henceforth under thy holy protection. For thine is the power and the glory, forever and ever. *So mote it be. Amen.*

* * * * * * * * *

BENEDICTION.

Let brotherly love continue. Be ye careful to entertain strangers. And may the God of peace and love be with us always. *So mote it be. Amen.*

Select Master.

NINTH DEGREE.

SYMBOLICAL DESIGN.

THE two virtues which it is particularly the symbolical design of the Select Master's degree to inculcate are secrecy and silence. They are, indeed,
called the cardinal virtues of a Select Master, because

the necessity of their practice is prominently set before the candidate in the legend, as well as in all the ceremonies of the degree. But these virtues constitute the very essence of all Masonic character · they are the safeguard of the institution, giving to it all its security and perpetuity, and are enforced by frequent admonitions in all the degrees, from the lowest to the highest. The Entered Apprentice begins his Masonic career by learning the duty of secrecy and silence. Hence it is appropriate that in that degree which is the consummation of initiation, in which the whole cycle of Masonic science is completed, the abstruse machinery of symbolism should be employed to impress the same important virtues on the mind of the neophyte.

The same principles of secrecy and silence existed in all the ancient mysteries and systems of worship. When Aristotle was asked what thing appeared to him to be most difficult of performance, he replied, " To be secret and silent."

" If we turn our eyes back to antiquity," says Calcott, " we shall find that the old Egyptians had so great a regard for silence and secrecy in the mysteries of their religion that they set up the god Harpocrates, to whom they paid peculiar honor and veneration ; who was represented with the right hand placed near the heart, and the left down by his side, covered with a skin before, full of eyes and ears ; to signify that of many things to be seen and heard few are to be published." *

Apuleius, who was an initiate in the mysteries of Isis, says: "By no peril will I ever be compelled to disclose to the uninitiated the things that I have had intrusted to me on condition of silence."

Lobeck, in his "Aglaophamus," has collected several examples of the reluctance with which the ancients approached a mystical subject, and the manner in which they shrunk from divulging any explanation or fable which had been related to them at the mysteries under the seal of secrecy and silence.

And lastly, in the school of Pythagoras these lessons were taught by the sage to his disciples. A novitiate of five years was imposed upon each pupil, which period was to be passed in total silence and religious and philosophical contemplation. And at length, when he was admitted to full fellowship in the society, an oath of secrecy was administered to him on the sacred tetractys, which was equivalent to the Jewish tetragrammaton.

Select Masters therefore work in secrecy and silence, that they may prepare and preserve the sacred deposits of truth until the time shall come for its full revelation. And so should all men do, working *now*, yet not for the present time alone, but

* Candid Disquisition of the Principles of Freemasonry.

that their labor may bring forth fruit in the future;
laboring here amid the foundations of the first temple of this transient life, that when their hours of
work are finished on earth, the deeds which they
have done may be brought to light, and the reward
be bestowed in the second temple of eternal life.

This is the true symbolism of the Select Master's
degree.

HISTORICAL SUMMARY.

The circumstances referred to in the degree of
Royal Master occurred during the building of the
first temple, and at a period of time which lies between the death of the Builder and the completion
of the edifice. Those referred to in the degree of
Select Master also occurred during the construction
of the Solomonic temple, but anterior to the Builder's death. Hence in the order of time the events
commemorated in the Select Master's degree took
place anterior to the occurrence of those which are
related in the degree of Royal Master, although in
the Masonic sequence the latter degree is conferred
before the former. This apparent anachronism is however reconciled by the explanation, that the secrets
of the Select Master's degree were not brought
to light until long after the existence of the Royal
Master's degree had been known and acknowledged.

In other words, to speak only from the traditional point of view, Select Masters had been designated, had performed the task for which they had been selected, and had closed their labors, without ever being openly recognized as a class in the temple of Solomon. Their occupation and their very existence, according to the legend, were unknown in the first temple. The Royal Master's degree, on the contrary, as there was no reason for concealment, was publicly conferred and acknowledged during the latter part of the construction of the temple of Solomon; whereas the degree of Select Master and the important incidents on which it was founded are not supposed to have been revealed to the Craft until the building of the Temple of Zerubbabel. Hence the Royal Master's degree is always conferred anterior to that of the Select Master.

OPENING OF THE COUNCIL

A Council of Select Masters consists of the following eight officers :—

---

* In some Councils the alarm is made by ♪♪♪ ♪♪♪ ♪♪ ♪ but the oldest rituals that I have seen agree in giving it as in the text, while all, both old and recent, concur that the pro-

THRICE ILLUSTRIOUS GRAND MASTER.
ILLUSTRIOUS HIRAM OF TYRE.
PRINCIPAL CONDUCTOR OF THE WORKS.
TREASURER.
RECORDER.
CAPTAIN OF THE GUARDS.
CONDUCTOR OF THE COUNCIL.
STEWARD.

Of these officers the first three represent respectively the three Grand Masters at the first temple.
The Steward, who acts as Sentinel or Tiler, represents Achisar, who is mentioned in 1 Kings iv. 6, as
being "over the household" of Solomon, or, as
Adam Clarke calls him, "the King's Chamberlain."
It is a mere fancy to suppose, as some ritualists
do, that the Treasurer represents Adoniram; the
Recorder, Jehoshaphat; and the Captain of the
Guards, Ahazariah, merely because corresponding
officers are said, in the fourth chapter of the first
book of Kings, to have been held by persons bearing
those names. But as none of them were inhabitants
of Gebal, the legend of the degree forbids us to

per battery is ♪♪♪♪♪♪♪♪ ♩ which appropriately refers
to the *eight* degrees already passed, and to the present *one*,
while the whole number of *nine* is one of the symbols of the
degree.

believe that these persons could have been Select Masters.

The position of these officers differs, in some respects, from those of the officers of a Council of Royal Masters. The Thrice Illustrious sits in the East before a triangular table. clothed in royal robes of purple, with a crown on his head and a scepter in his hand. The King of Tyre sits on his right, clothed in the same manner with purple robes, crown and scepter, and also before a triangular table. The Principal Conductor of the Works sits on his left, clothed in yellow robes, with a gavel in his hand and before a triangular table, on which is a triangular plate of gold, on which the Ineffable Name is inscribed. On each of the tables is also placed a small trowel. The Treasurer is seated in the North, the Recorder in the South, and the Captain of the Guards, the Conductor of the Council, and the Steward, respectively, occupy the positions and perform the duties of the Senior and Junior Deacons and the Tiler of a symbolic Lodge.

The symbolic colors of a Select Master, like those of a Royal Master, are black and red, but the symbolism is different. The black is significant of the secrecy, silence, and darkness in which the Select Masters performed their labors, and the red, of their fervency and zeal. Hence the apron and collar of a Select Master must be black, lined and

edged with red. The apron should be of a triangular form, in allusion to the sacred delta. In some
Councils it is decorated with nine stars, three
placed in each angle of the apron, and in the
center the letters I. S., or what would be better,
the equivalent Hebrew letters ם. ׳. The jewel of
a Select Master is a silver trowel within a triangle
of the same metal, and this worn suspended from
collar by every officer and member.

The place of meeting represents a secret vault or
crypt beneath the temple; and hence that part of
the Masonic system which refers to the degrees of
Royal and Select Master is usually called " Cryptic
Masonry."

A Council of Select Masters is supposed to consist
of neither more nor less than twenty-seven, although
a smaller number, if not less than nine, is competent
to proceed to work or business. The nine should be
exclusive of the Steward, who is not considered as
one of the Council.

A candidate is said to be " chosen as a Select
Master."

At the opening of the Council use is made of the
following

PRAYER.

May the Supreme Grand Master graciously
preside over all our counsels, and direct, ap-

prove, and bless all our labors. May our professions as Masons be the rule of our conduct as men. May our secret retreat ever be the resort of the *just* and *merciful;* the seat of the moral virtues, and the home of the *select. So mote it be. Amen.*

RECEPTION.

The following passages of Scripture are deemed applicable to the reception into this degree, as explanatory of the events which it records :—

I KINGS iv. 1, 5, 6.

So King Solomon was King over all Israel. And Azariah, the son of Nathan, was over the officers: and Zabud, the son of Nathan, was principal officer and the King's friend : and Ahishar was over the household: and Adoni· ram, the son of Abda, was over the tribute.

I KINGS v. 17, 18.

And the King commanded, and they brought great stones, costly stones and hewed stones, to lay the foundation of the house. And Solomon's builders and Hiram's builders did hew them, and the stone-squarers :* so

---

* The word here translated "stone-squarers," is in the original גבלים or *Giblim.* See the explanation on a subseqnent page.

they prepared timber and stones to build the house.

1 KINGS vii. 18, 14.

And King Solomon sent and fetched Hiram out of Tyre. He was a widow's son, of the tribe of Naphtali, and his father was a man of Tyre, a worker in brass: and he was filled with wisdom and understanding, and cunning to work all works in brass. And he came to King Solomon and worked all his work.

THE CIRCLE OF PERFECTION.

The ceremonies of reception into the degree of Select Master are of a compound nature, because they refer to two entirely distinct events. The earliest monitorial instruction that was given to the public on the subject of this degree, states that it rationally accounts for the concealment and preservation of those essentials of the craft which were brought to light at the erection of the second temple, and which lay concealed from the Masonic eye for four hundred and seventy years.

The inculcation of this doctrine—the imparting of this knowledge—undoubtedly constitutes the important object of the degree. It is because of its thus rationally accounting for the concealment and preservation of these fundamental mysteries of Freemasonry, filling up an hiatus between the Master's and the Royal Arch degrees, that the initiates into the Select Master's degree are said to have "passed the circle of perfection."

The idea of comparing the progress of Masonic science to a circle, with whomsoever it originated, is a good one. The true signification of the phrase may be readily illustrated. Let us, then, suppose that the science of Freemasonry, or, in more definite words, the science of Masonic symbolism, is represented by a circle. This circle will be divided into three portions or arcs : One arc will be occupied by the degrees of the Lodge, or Ancient Craft Masonry ; another by the degrees of the Chapter, or Royal Arch Masonry ; and the third by the degrees of the Council, or Cryptic Masonry. Now, if a neophyte begins at any point of the circle, and passes over one-third of its circumference, he will arrive at the Master's degree, and will then discover that, so far, the consummation of his Masonic labor is to know only that that for which he has been striving has been LOST, and, instead of the key to all Masonic science, he receives only a *substitute* for truth.

Dissatisfied with this, let him, in his further search, proceed through another arc, or third of the circumference of the Masonic circle, and he will arrive at the Royal Arch degree. Here, in this second arc, that key which had been LOST in the first arc is FOUND.

But the circle has not yet been completed. It is true that the neophyte now knows that the lost has been found. He is perhaps even put in possession of the sacred treasure. But the process by which the restoration was accomplished is still unknown to him, and all the events of Masonic mythical history which form the links between the loss and the recovery, and all the sublime symbolism which is connected with these events, are withheld from him. He knows what he has obtained, but he knows not why nor how he obtained it. To acquire this knowledge he passes through the remaining arc, and, by arriving at the degree of Select Master, consummates and perfects his knowledge of the representative symbol of Divine Truth, and thus passes the circle of perfection in Masonic science.

But the same early monitorial instruction informs us that in this degree is exemplified an instance of justice and mercy by our ancient patron, toward one of the Craft who was led to disobey his commands by an over-zealous attachment for the institution. The event here referred to, however striking may be its dramatic effect, is really totally unconnected with the true symbolism of the degree. It is merely an interesting episode, which was introduced into the body of the Masonic epic by some ingenious but modern ritualist. So little is it really connected with the mythical symbolism of the degree, that it might actually be dismissed from the ceremonies of initiation without in the slightest manner affecting the great design of the degree, or in any way impairing the completeness of that circle of perfection to which we have just alluded. The science of the degree, as connected with the *loss* and the *recovery* of the truth, would not be at all impaired by its removal from the ritual. But it has been so long retained as a part of the ceremonial observance, that it could not at this late day be dispensed with, and it must therefore remain, like a superfluous stone in the edifice, which adds no strength to the building; a ceremony in Masonry without a symbolism, or at most only intended to exemplify the union and the practice of the two virtues, *mercy* and *justice.*

THE ALTAR.

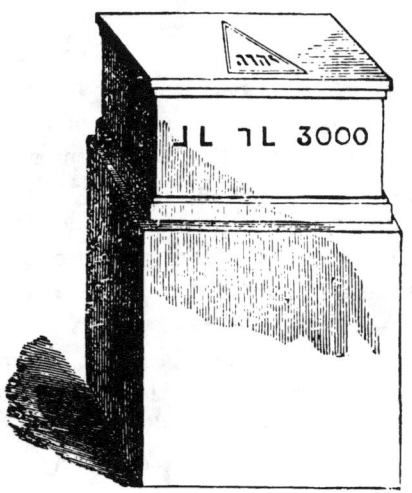

The Altar, in a Council of Royal and Select Masters, represents the celebrated Stone of Foundation in the temple, a notice of which will be found in a subsequent part of this volume. It should, therefore, unlike other Masonic altars, be constructed to represent a cubical stone without other ornaments, and on it should be deposited the Substitute Ark. As the Masonic legend places the Stone of Foundation in the Sanctum Sanctorum of the second temple, but immediately beneath it in the first, and

as that point is represented by the ninth arch in a
Council of Select Masters, it is evident that during
a reception, at least, the altar should be placed
within that arch, and not, as is too often done, outside of it, or even in the center of the room.

THE SECRET VAULT.

Considered simply as an historical question, there
can be no doubt of the existence of immense vaults
beneath the superstructure of the original temple of
Solomon. Prime, Robison, and other writers who
in recent times have described the topography of
Jerusalem, speak of the existence of these struc-
tures, which they visited, and, in some instances,
carefully examined.

After the destruction of Jerusalem by Titus, the
Roman Emperor Hadrian erected on the site of the
" House of the Lord " a temple of Venus, which
in its turn was destroyed, and the place subsequently
became a depository of all manner of filth. But
the Caliph Omar, after his conquest of Jerusalem, sought out the ancient site, and, having
caused it to be cleansed of its impurities, he directed
a mosque to be erected on the rock which rises in
the center of the mountain. Fifty years afterward
the Sultan Abd-el-Meluk displaced the edifice of
Omar, and erected that splendid building which

remains to this day, and is still incorrectly called by Christians the mosque of Omar, but known to Mussulmans as El-kubbet-es-Sukhrah, or the Dome of the Rock. This is supposed to occupy the exact site of the original Solomonic temple, and is viewed with equal reverence by Jews and Mahommedans, the former of whom, says Mr. Prime, " have a faith that the ark is within its bosom now."[*]

Bartlett,[†] in describing a vault beneath this mosque of Omar, says: " Beneath the dome, at the southeast angle of the temple wall, conspicuous from all points, is a small subterraneous place of prayer, forming the entrance to the extensive vaults which support the level platform of the mosque above."

Dr. Barclay[‡] describes, in many places of his interesting topography of Jerusalem, the vaults and subterranean chambers which are to be found beneath the site of the old temple.

Conformably with this historical account is the Talmudical legend, in which the Jewish Rabbins state that, in preparing the foundations of the temple, the workmen discovered a subterranean vault sustained by seven arches, rising from as many pairs

---

* Prime.   Tent Life in the Holy Land, p. 188.
† Walks about the City of Jerusalem, p. 170.
‡ City of the Great King.

of pillars. This vault escaped notice at the destruction of Jerusalem, in consequence of its being filled with rubbish. The legend adds, that Josiah, foreseeing the destruction of the temple, commanded the Levites to deposit the ark of the covenant in this vault, where it was found by some of the workmen of Zerubbabel, at the building of the second temple.

In the earliest ages the cave or vault was deemed sacred. The first worship was in cave temples, which were either natural, or formed by art to resemble the excavations of nature. Of such great extent was this practice of subterranean worship by the nations of antiquity, that many of the forms of heathen temples, as well as the naves, aisles, and chancels of churches subsequently built for Christian worship, are said to owe their origin to the religious use of caves.

From this, too, arose the fact, that the initiation into the ancient mysteries was almost always performed in subterranean edifices ; and when the place of initiation, as in some of the Egyptian temples, was really above ground, it was so constructed as to give to the neophyte the appearance, in its approaches and its internal structure, of a vault. As the great doctrine taught in the mysteries was the resurrection from the dead, as *to die* and *to be initiated* were synonymous terms, it was deemed proper that there should be some formal resemblance between a descent into the grave and a descent into the place of initiation. "Happy is the man," says the Greek poet Pindar, "who descends beneath the hollow earth, having beheld these mysteries, for he knows the end as well as the divine origin of life;" and in a like spirit Sophocles exclaims, "Thrice happy are they who descend to the shades below after having beheld these sacred rites, for they alone have life in Hades, while all others suffer there every kind of evil."

The vault was, therefore, in the ancient mysteries, symbolic of the grave; for initiation was symbolic of death, where alone Divine Truth is to be found. The Masons have adopted the same idea. They teach that death is but the beginning of life; that if the first or evanescent temple of our transitory life be on the surface, we must descend into the *secret vault* of death before we can find that sacred deposit of truth which is to adorn our second temple of eternal life. Looking, therefore, to this reference of initiation to that subterranean house of our last dwelling, we significantly speak of the place of initiation as "the secret vault, where reign silence, secrecy, and darkness." It is in this sense of an entrance through the grave into eternal life, that the Select Master is to view the recondite but beautiful symbolism of the secret vault. Like every other myth and allegory of Masonry, the historical relation may be true or it may be false; it may be founded on fact or the invention of imagination; the lesson is still there, and the symbolism teaches it exclusive of the history.

ACHISHAR.

This is the person named in the First Book of Kings, iv. 6, under the name of *Ahishar*, and there described as being "over the household" of King Solomon. Adam Clarke describes him as "the king's chamberlain," but the original title of *al-bait* properly signifies, as Gesenius remarks, "the dispenser or steward who had charge of the household affairs and of the other servants." The very same words are used in Genesis xliv. 1, and there translated "the steward of his house." Achishar is therefore properly described in this degree as the steward of the household.

As to the legend of his conduct and his punishment, it has no known foundation in history, and may be considered simply as a mythical symbol.

IZABUD.

This, like Achishar, is an historical personage, although the events recorded of him as peculiar to this degree are altogether legendary. The word is one of those corruptions of Hebrew names unfortunately too common in Masonry. The true name is Zabud; and he is mentioned in the First Book of Kings iv. 5, where it is said, "Zabud, the son of Nathan, was principal officer and the King's friend." Kitto* says of Zabud and of his brother Azariah, that their advancement in the household of King Solomon "may doubtless be ascribed not only to the young king's respect for the venerable prophet (their father), who had been his instructor, but to the friendship he had contracted with his sons during the course of education. The office, or rather honor of 'friend of the King' we find in all the despotic governments of the East. It gives high power, without the public responsibility which the holding of a regular office in the state necessarily imposes. It implies the possession of the utmost confidence of, and familiar intercourse with, the monarch, to whose person 'the friend' at all times has access, and whose influence is therefore often far greater, even in matters of state, than that of the recognized ministers of government."

It is scarcely necessary to say how closely all this has been observed in the legend of the Select Master's degree. It is time, however, that the word *Zabud* should be substituted for the corrupt form *Izabud*, now constantly used.

* Cyclopedia of Biblical Literature, in voc. *Zabua.*

CHESED.

This word, which is most generally corrupted into HESED, is the Hebrew חסד, and signifies *mercy*. Hence it very appropriately refers to that act of kindness and compassion which is commemorated in this degree.

ISH SODI.

This expression is composed of the two Hebrew words, שי ISH, and סוד, SOD. The first of these words, ISH, means *a man*, and SOD signifies primarily *a couch* on which one reclines. Hence ISH SODI would mean, first, *a man of my couch*, one who reclines with me on the same seat, an indication of great familiarity and confidence. Thence followed the secondary meaning given to SOD of familiar intercourse, consultation, or intimacy. Job (xix. 19) applies it in this sense when, using MATI, a word synonymous with ISH, he speaks of MATI SODI in the passage which the common version has translated thus: "all my *inward friends* abhorred me," but which the marginal interpretation has more correctly rendered, "all the men of my secret." *Ish Sodi*, therefore, in this degree very clearly means, *a man of my intimate counsel, a man of my choice,* one selected to share with me a secret task or labor.

Such was the position of every Select Master to King Solomon, and in this view those are not wrong who have interpreted *Ish Sodi* as meaning a *Select Master*.

THE SUBSTITUTE ARK.

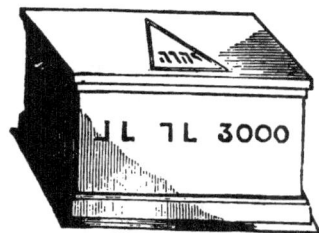

The Ark or Coffer which necessarily constitutes a part of the paraphernalia of a Council of Select Masters, is the same as that which forms a part of the furniture of a Chapter of the Royal Arch. But it must be distinctly understood that neither of these represents that Ark of the Covenant which had been constructed in the wilderness by Moses, Aholiab, and Bezaleel, which had been placed in the tabernacle, and afterwards, at the dedication of the Temple of Solomon was removed to the Holy of Holies. The later history of this ark is buried in obscurity. It is supposed that upon the destruction of the first temple by the Chaldeans, it was carried to Babylon among the other sacred utensils which became the

spoil of the conquerors. But of its subsequent fate
all traces have been lost. It is, however, certain
that it was not brought back to Jerusalem by Zerubbabel. The Talmudists say that there were five
things which were the glory of the first temple that
were wanting in the second; namely, the Ark of the
Covenant, the Shechinah, or Divine Presence, the
Urim and Thummim, the holy fire upon the altar, and
the spirit of prophecy. The Rev. Salem Towne,* it
is true, has endeavored to prove, by a very ingenious
argument, that the original Ark of the Covenant
was concealed by Josiah or by others, at some time
previous to the destruction of Jerusalem, and that it
was afterwards, at the building of the second temple, discovered and brought to light. But such a
theory is entirely at variance with all the legends of
the degree of Select Master and of Royal Arch
Masonry. To admit it would lead to endless con-
fusion and contradictions in the traditions of the
order. It is besides in conflict with the opinions of
the Rabbinical writers and every Hebrew scholar.
Josephus and the Rabbins allege that in the second
temple the Holy of Holies was empty, or contained
only the stone of foundation which marked the place
which the ark should have occupied.

But Prideaux,† on the authority of Lightfoot,

* System of Speculative Masonry, p. 222 et seq.
† Old and New Testament Connected, vol. i p.

contends that as an ark was indispensable to the Israelitish worship, there was in the second temple an ark which had been expressly made for the purpose of supplying the place of the first or original ark, and which, without possessing any of its prerogatives or honors, was of precisely thes ame shape and dimensions, and was deposited in the same place.

These are historical problems which it would be vain for us to attempt at this late day to solve. The Masonic legend, however, whether authentic or not, is simple and connected. It teaches that there was an ark in the second temple, but that it was neither the Ark of the Covenant, which had been in the Holy of Holies of the first temple, nor one that had been constructed as a substitute for it after the building of the second temple. It was that ark which is presented to us in the Select Master's degree, and which, being an exact copy of the Mosaical ark, and intended to replace it in case of its loss, is best known to Freemasons as the *Substitute Ark.*

GIBLEMITES.

This is peculiarly a Masonic form for the more usual word *Giblites.* It designates the inhabitants of Gebal, a city of Phœnicia, on the shore of the Mediterranean, and under Mount Lebanon. The Hebrew word is גבלים, *Giblim*, and is to be found

in 1 Kings v. 18, where it is translated, in our com
mon version, "stone-squarers" in the following passage: "And Solomon's builders and Hiram's builders did hew them, and the stone-squarers; so they
prepared timber and stones to build the house."
The translation would be more correctly thus:
"And Solomon's builders and Hiram's builders and
the Giblemites did hew them."

The Giblemites, or inhabitants of Gebal, were
subject to the King of Tyre, and were distinguished
for their skill as builders. The town of Gebal was
called Byblos by the Greeks, and was celebrated as
the principal seat of the worship of Adonis, whose
mysteries, and the initiation accompanying it, more
nearly resembled, in its symbolism and allegorical
teaching, the initiation into Masonry than any other
of the ancient rites. It is not, therefore, unnatural
to suppose that the Giblemites held a higher place
in the confidence of King Solomon than any other
of the Temple builders.

THE NINE ARCHES.

Of all the superstitious notions which prevailed
among the ancient philosophers, there was none
more prevalent than that which attributed a mystical meaning and a divine virtue to numbers. Nor
did the idea die with antiquity. It was a favorite

theory of many of the Christian Fathers, and even as late as the sixteenth century we find Cornelius Agrippa[*] asserting that "there lies wonderful efficacy and virtue in numbers, as well for good as for evil." The doctrine was especially taught in the school of Pythagoras, and afterwards by the Cabbalists, whence it has evidently descended to Freemasonry, of whose symbolical science it constitutes an interesting portion. But the numeral symbolism of Masonry very materially differs from that of the Pythagoreans as well as the Cabbalista.

With the Masons, odd numbers alone are considered mystical, which was according to the ancient doctrine, where it was taught that odd numbers were pleasing to the gods.[†] Hence *three, five, seven,* and *nine,* are deemed Masonic numbers. *Three* is the foundation of the Masonic symbolism of numbers, because it is the first odd number after unity, and it is particularly applicable to the lower degrees. When we ascend to the higher grades, *nine* comes into play as the square of three, and *twenty-seven,* which is the cube of three, and lastly *eighty-one* which is the square of *nine.*

The number *nine* is the sacred number of the Select degree, which, however, also refers to *twenty-*

---

[*] Philos. Occult., Lib. II. Cap. iii.

[†] Numero deus impare gaudet. Virg. Ecl. viii. 75.

seven, simply because that is the product of *nine* multiplied by *three*.

Nine was called by the Pythagoreans *teïeios*, or the number of completion, and as such it is appropriate to that degree which professes to complete the circle of Masonic science. But the lecture of the Select Master teaches us that the number *nine* alludes to the nine attributes of the Deity, which are said to be : 1. Beauty. 2. Wisdom. 3. Power. 4. Eternity. 5. Infinity. 6. Omniscience. 7. Justice. 8. Mercy. 9. Perfection.

THE STONE OF FOUNDATION.

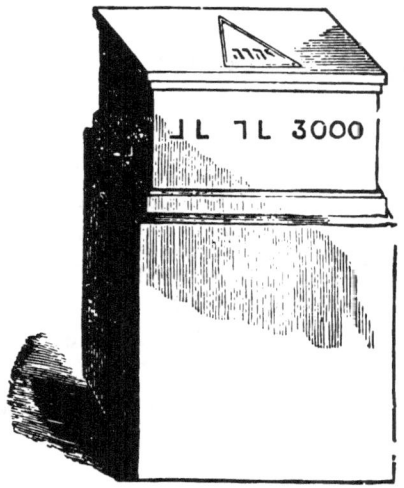

The Stone of Foundation, which in this degree is represented by the altar on which is placed the Substitute Ark, constitutes one of the most important as well as abstruse of the symbols of Freemasonry. It is, it is true, scarcely alluded to, except in a very general way, in the primitive degrees of Ancient Craft Masonry, but is peculiarly appropriate to the Royal Arch, and especially to the degree of Select Master, where it is really the most essential symbol of the degree

The Stone of Foundation must, however, be distinguished, both in its symbolism and in its legendary history, from other stones which play an important part in the Masonic ritual, but which are entirely distinct from it.   Such are the *corner-stone*, which was always placed in the northeast corner of the building about to be erected, and to which such a beautiful reference is made in the ceremonies of the first degree; or the *keystone*, which constitutes an interesting part of the Mark Master's degree; or, lastly, the *cape-stone*, upon which all the ritual of the Most Excellent Master's degree is founded. These are all, in their proper places, highly interesting and instructive symbols, but have no connection whatever with the Stone of Foundation, whose symbolism it is our present object to discuss.   Nor, although the Stone of Foundation is said, for peculiar reasons, to have been of a cubical form, must it be confounded with that stone called by the continental Masons the *cubical stone*—the *pierre cubique* of the French, and the *cubik stein* of the German Masons, but which in the English system is known as the *perfect ashlar*.   This has a legendary history and a symbolic signification which are peculiar to itself, and which, differing from the history and meaning which belong to these other stones, particularly connect it with the degree of Select Master.

The Stone of Foundation is supposed, in the

science of Masonic symbolism, to have been a stone placed at one time within the foundations of the first temple, or that of Solomon, and afterward, during the building of the second temple, transported to the Holy of Holies. It was in form a perfect cube, and had inscribed upon its upper face, within a delta or triangle, the sacred tetragrammaton, or Ineffable Name of God.

Oliver, speaking with the solemnity of a historian, says that Solomon thought that he had rendered the house of God worthy, so far as human adornment could effect, for the dwelling of God, " when he had placed the celebrated Stone of Foundation, on which the sacred name was mystically engraven, with solemn ceremonies, in that sacred depository on Mount Moriah, along with the foundations of Dan and Asher, the center of the Most Holy Place, where the ark was overshadowed by the shekinah of God."

The Hebrew Talmudists, who thought as much of this stone and had as many legends concerning it as the Masonic Talmudists, called it *eben shatijah*, or " Stone of Foundation," because, as they said, it had been laid by Jehovah, as the foundation of the world, and hence the apocryphal book of Enoch speaks of the " stone which supports the corners of the earth."

The Masonic legends of the Stone of Foundation are very numerous, and many of them contradictory and unsatisfactory. The series of legends which is now very generally adopted by Masonic scholars is that which commences with the patriarch Enoch, who is supposed to have been the first consecrator of the Stone of Foundation.

This legend in full is as follows: Enoch, under the inspiration of the Most High, and in obedience to the instructions which he had received in a vision, built a temple under ground on Mount Moriah, and dedicated it to God. His son, Methuselah, constructed the building, although he was not acquainted with his father's motives for the erection. This temple consisted of nine vaults, situated perpendicularly beneath each other, and communicating by apertures left in each vault.

Enoch then caused a triangular plate of gold to be made, each side of which was a cubit long; he enriched it with the most precious stones, and incrusted the plate upon a stone of agate of the same form. On the plate he engraved the true name of God, or the tetragrammaton, and, placing it on a cubical stone, known thereafter as the Stone of Foundation, he deposited the whole within the lowest arch.

When this subterranean building was completed, he made a door of stone, and attaching to it a ring of iron, by which it might be occasionally raised, he placed it over the opening of the uppermost arch, and so covered it that the aperture could not be discovered. Enoch himself was not permitted to enter

it but once a year, and on the deaths of Enoch,
Methuselah, and Lamech, and the destruction of the
world by the deluge, all knowledge of the vault or
subterranean temple and of the Stone of Foundation
with the Ineffable Name inscribed upon it, was lost
for ages to the world.

At the building of the first temple of Jerusalem
the Stone of Foundation again makes its appearance.
According to the legend, when King Solomon was
digging the foundations of the temple he discovered
this stone of Enoch, which for wise purposes he
deposited in a secure and secret place, that the Ineffable Name upon it might be preserved for future
times.

The Foundation Stone of Masonry appears to be
intimately connected with the stone worship of the
ancients. History affords abundant examples which
prove that the worship of a cubical stone formed an
important feature of the religions of the primitive
nations. But Cudworth, Bryant, Faber, and all
other distinguished writers who have treated the
subject, have long since established the theory that
the Pagan religions were eminently symbolic. Thus,
to use the language of Dudley, the pillar of stone
" was adopted as a symbol of strength and firmness—
a symbol, also, of the divine power, and, by a ready
inference, a symbol or idol of the Deity himself."
And this symbolism is confirmed by Phurnutus,

whom Toland quotes as saying that the god Hermes was represented without hands or feet, being a cubical stone, because the cubical figure betokened his solidity and stability.

Profane and Masonic history combined seem to establish the following series of facts: First, that there was a very general prevalence among the earliest nations of antiquity of the worship of stones as the representatives of Deity; secondly, that in almost every ancient temple there was a legend of a sacred or mystical stone; thirdly, that this legend is found in the Masonic system; and, lastly, that the mystical stone there has received the name of the "Stone of Foundation."

Now, as in all the other systems the stone is admitted to be symbolic, and the tradition connected with it mystical, we are compelled to assume the same predicates of the Masonic stone. It, too, is symbolic, and its legend a myth or an allegory.

The fact that the mystical stone in all the ancient religions was a symbol of the Deity, leads us necessarily to the conclusion that the Stone of Foundation was also a symbol of Deity. And this symbolic idea is strengthened by the tetragrammaton or sacred name of God that was inscribed upon it. This Ineffable Name sanctifies the stone upon which it is engraved as the symbol of the Grand Architect. It takes from it its heathen signification as an idol, and consecrates it to the worship of the true God.

The predominant idea of the Deity, in the Masonic system, connects him with his creative and formative power. God is to the Freemason *Al-Gabil*, as the Arabians called him, that is, *The Builder;* or, as expressed in his Masonic title, the *Grand Architect of the Universe*, by common consent abbreviated in the formula G A O T U. Now, it is evident that no symbol could so appropriately suit Him in this character as the Stone of Foundation, upon which He is allegorically supposed to have erected His world. Such a symbol closely connects the creative work of God, as a pattern and exemplar, with the workman's erection of his temporal building on a similar foundation-stone.

But this Masonic idea is still further to be extended. The great object of all Masonic labor is *divine truth*. The search for the *lost word* is the search for truth. But divine truth is a term synonymous with God. The Ineffable Name is a symbol of truth, because God, and God alone, is truth. It is properly a Scriptural idea. The Book of Psalms abounds with this sentiment. Thus it is said that the truth of the Lord "reacheth unto the clouds," and that "His truth endureth unto all generations." If, then, God is truth, and the Stone of Foundation is the Masonic symbol of

God, it follows that it must also be the symbol of divine truth.

When we have arrived at this point in our speculations, we are ready to show how all the myths and legends of the Stone of Foundation may be rationally explained as parts of that beautiful "science of morality, veiled in allegory and illustrated by symbols," which is the acknowledged definition of Freemasonry.

In the Masonic system there are two temples; the first temple, in which the degrees of Ancient Craft Masonry are concerned, and the second temple, with which the higher degrees, and especially the Royal Arch, are related. The first temple is symbolic of the present life; the second temple is symbolic of the life to come. The first temple, the present life, must be destroyed; on its foundations the second temple, the life eternal, must be built.

But the mystical stone was placed by King Solomon in the foundations of the first temple. That is to say, the first temple of our present life must be built on the sure foundation of divine truth, "for other foundation can no man lay."

But although the present life is necessarily built upon the foundation of truth, yet we never thoroughly attain it in this sublunary sphere. The Foundation Stone is concealed in the first temple, and the Master Mason knows it not. He has not the true word. He receives only a substitute.

But in the second temple of the future life we have passed from the grave, which had been the end of our labors in the first. We have removed the rubbish, and have found that Stone of Foundation which had been hitherto concealed from our eyes. We now throw aside the substitute for truth, which had contented us in the former temple, and the brilliant effulgence of the tetragrammaton and the Stone of Foundation are discovered, and thenceforth we are the possessors of the true word—of divine truth. And in this way the Stone of Foundation, or divine truth, concealed in the first temple, but discovered and brought to light in the second, will explain that passage of the Apostle: "For now we see through a glass darkly; but then, face to face: now I know in part; but then shall I know even as also I am known."

And so we arrive at this result, that the Masonic Stone of Foundation, so conspicuous in the degree of Select Master, is a symbol of divine truth, upon which all Speculative Masonry is built; and the legends and traditions which refer to it are intended to describe, in an allegorical way, the progress of truth in the soul, the search for which is a Mason's labor; and the discovery of which is to be his reward.

CHARGE

TO A NEWLY INITIATED SELECT MASTER.

COMPANION:—Having attained to this degree, you have passed the *circle of perfection* in ancient Masonry. In the capacity of a Select Master, you must be sensible that your obligations are increased in proportion to your privileges. Let it be your constant care to prove yourself worthy of the confidence that has been reposed in you, and of the high honor that has been conferred upon you in admitting you to this select degree. Let uprightness and integrity attend your steps; let *justice* and *mercy* mark your conduct; let *fervency* and *zeal* stimulate you in the discharge of the various duties incumbent on you; but suffer not an idle and impertinent *curiosity* to lead you astray or betray you into danger. Be deaf to every insinuation which would have a tendency to weaken your resolution, or tempt you to an act of disobedience. Be voluntarily *dumb* and *blind* when the exercise of those faculties would endanger the peace of your mind or the probity of your conduct; and let *silence* and *secrecy,* those cardinal virtues of a Select Master, on all necessary occasions be scrupulously observed. By a steady adherence to the important instructions contained in this degree, you will merit the approbation of the select number with whom you are associated, and will enjoy the high satisfaction of having acted well your part in the important enterprise in which you are engaged; and after having *wrought your regular hours,* may you be permitted to participate in all the privileges of a Select Master, and to enter the Celestial Council, where you will behold that divine *Stone of Foundation* on which rests *Eternal Truth.*

CLOSING OF A COUNCIL.

In closing a Council of Select Masters use is made of the following

CHARGE.

COMPANIONS :—Being about to quit this sacred retreat to mix again with the world, let us not forget, amid the cares and vicissitudes of active life, the bright example of sincere friendship, so beautifully illustrated in the lives of the founders of this degree. Let us take the lesson home with us, and may it strengthen the bands of fraternal love between us, unite our hearts to duty, and our desires to wisdom. Let us exercise Charity, cherish Hope, and walk in Faith. And may that moral principle which is the mystic cement of our fellowship remain with and bless us.

Response: So mote it be. Amen.

4

Super-Excellent Master.

SUPER-EXCELLENT MASTER.

HISTORY AND SYMBOLISM.

THE degree of Super-Excellent Master certainly has no connection, in its history or its symbolism, with the Royal and Select degrees, nor was it ever, until it was very recently introduced by a few Councils in some of the Northern and Western States, considered as forming any part of the work of a Council. I do not myself acknowledge its legitimacy as a degree of Cryptic Masonry, and I seriously object to its introduction into the Council, because it destroys the symmetry of the rite which very properly closes with the ninth degree. A description of it is, however, inserted in this Manual, because, although I deem it misplaced, it has nevertheless been adopted, and is worked by many Councils, and is, withal, an interesting degree, and conveys some valuable information.

But although the introduction of the degree, into the Council work is of very recent date, being unnoticed by any writer who has hitherto compiled a Masonic monitor, the degree itself can boast of a

much longer existence. It has always been in possession of the Supreme Councils of the Ancient and
Accepted Rite, and was frequently conferred by the
Inspectors-General as a "detached" or honorary
degree.* It is not, however, a degree that has been
very generally known to Masonic writers. Lenning
makes no allusion to it in his very copious "Ency-
clopadie der Freimaurerei," nor is it to be found in
the catalogue of several hundred degrees given by
Thory in his "Acta Latomorum." But, on the
other hand, Dr. Oliver,† in his "Landmarks,"
describes the degree with such completeness as

---

* Dalcho, in his "Orations," says, while speaking of the
thirty-three degrees of the Ancient and Accepted Rite:
"Besides those degrees which are in regular succession, most
of the Inspectors are in possession of a number of detached
degrees, given in different parts of the world, and which
they generally communicate, free of expense, to those brethren who are high enough to understand them."—*Dalcho's
'Orations*, Charleston, 1801, p. 68. It was in this way that,
twenty years ago, I myself received the degree from the hands
of Illustrious Brother Alex. McDonald, at that time Grand
Commander of the Supreme Council for the Southern Jurisdiction of the United States, who at the same time presented
me with a ritual, copied by him from a much older one in
the possession of Brother Roche, a former member of the
Supreme Council.

† Historical Landmarks of Freemasonry, vol. ii. p. 187. I
mention the name of this venerable patriarch almost at the

to demonstrate that he must have seen or been in possession of its ritual precisely as it is practiced in this country.

The Masonic legend of the degree of Super-Excellent Master refers to circumstances which occurred on the last day of the siege of Jerusalem by Nebuzaradan, the captain of the Chaldean army, who had been sent by Nebuchadnezzar to destroy the city and temple, as a just punishment of the Jewish king Zedekiah, for his perfidy and rebellion. It occupies, therefore, precisely that point of time which is embraced in that part of the Royal Arch degree which represents the destruction of the temple, and the carrying of the Jews in captivity to Babylon. It is, in fact, an exemplification and extension of that part of the Royal Arch degree.

As to the symbolic design of the degree, it is very evident that its legend and ceremonies are intended to inculcate that important Masonic virtue, fidelity to vows. Zedekiah, the wicked king of Judah, is, by the modern ritualists who have symbolized the degree, adopted very appropriately as the symbol of perfidy, and the severe but well-deserved punishment which was inflicted on him by the king of

very moment that the melancholy tidings of his death have reached me. As one honored with his friendship and grateful for his instructions, I dedicate this sentence to the memory of the most learned and enthusiastic of Masons.

Babylon is set forth in the lecture as a great moral lesson, whose object is to warn the recipient of the fatal effects that will ensue from a violation of his sacred obligations.

OPENING OF THE COUNCIL.

A Council of Super-Excellent Masters consists of the following eleven officers:—

MOST EXCELLENT KING.

COMPANION GEDALIAH.

FIRST KEEPER OF THE TEMPLE.

SECOND KEEPER OF THE TEMPLE.

THIRD KEEPER OF THE TEMPLE.

CAPTAIN OF THE GUARDS.

FIRST HERALD.

SECOND HERALD.

THIRD HERALD.

TREASURER.

SECRETARY.

The Most Excellent King represents Zedekiah, the twentieth and last king of Judah. He is seated in the East. Gedaliah is seated in the West, except during a reception, when he assumes a station in

front of the King. The First Keeper of the Temple
is seated in front of the West. The Second and
Third on the left of the West, and near the door of
preparation. The Captain of the Guards is seated
on the right hand of the King: the Three Heralds
are on the outside of the door, and the Treasurer and
Secretary occupy the usual positions of those officers
in other Masonic bodies. There are also three Guards
who attend the King as an escort, but they are not per-
manent officers, and are assigned no definite position.

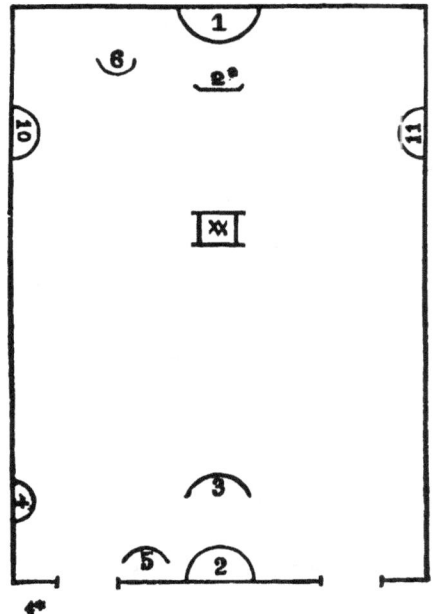

In this diagram 1 represents the seat of the King;
2 that of Gedaliah, and 2* his seat at a reception;
3, 4 and 5 the stations of the First, Second, and
Third Keepers of the Temple; 6 that of the Captain of the Guards; 10 that of the Treasurer; and
11 that of the Secretary.

RECEPTION.

The following passages of Scripture are appropriately read in the course of a reception into this
degree.

LAMENTATIONS 1. 1.

How does the city sit solitary, that was full
of people: how is she become as a widow!
she that was great among the nations and
princess among the provinces, how is she
become tributary! She weepeth sore in the
night, and her tears are on her cheeks: among
all her lovers she has none to comfort her: all
her friends have dealt treacherously with her,
they are become her enemies.

In many Councils, during a part of the reception
the following hymn is sung, accompanied with appropriate and impressive ceremonies.

HYMN.

By Babel's stream we sit and weep,
 Our tears for Zion flow;
Our harps on drooping willows sleep,
 Our hearts are filled with woe.

Our walls no more resound with praise,
 Our Temple foes destroy;
Judea's courts no more upraise
 Triumphant songs of joy.

Here mourning toil and captive bands,
 Our feasts and Sabbaths cease;
Our tribes dispersed through distant lands
 And hopeless of release.

But should the ever-gracious power
To us propitious be;
Chaldeans shall our race restore,
And Kings proclaim us free.

THE DESTRUCTION OF THE TEMPLE.

The destruction of the temple which had been built by King Solomon is the important event that is recorded in the legend of this degree. This was not the result of a single hostile act, but was brought about after a series of wars and sieges, which, with brief intervals of peace and prosperity, lasted for one hundred and fifty years, and finally culminated not only in the destruction of the city of Jerusalem, its holy temple, and all its magnificent palaces and dwellings, but also in the total annihilation of the kingdoms of Israel and Judah. About the year 741 B. C., which was two hundred and sixty-three years after the building of the temple, and in the reign of Ahaz, king of Judah, an invasion of Palestine was made by Tiglath-pileser, king of Assyria, who carried off the pastoral population that lived beyond the river Jordan, together with the tribes of Zebulon and Naphtali. His successor, Shalmanezer, continued these predatory incursions, and after having made Hoshea, the king of Israel, tributary to Assyria, when the tribute was withheld he attacked and reduced Samaria, in the year 721 b. c., and carried the remnant of the ten tribes, which constituted the Israelitish monarchy, into Assyria and Media, whence they never returned. This was the end of the kingdom of Israel.

But the kingdom of Judah still remained, con sisting of the tribes of Judah and Benjamin, the capital of which was the city of Jerusalem.

Less than a century after the extinction of the kingdom of Israel, Nebuchadnezzar, the Chaldean monarch, commenced those hostile aggressions upon the kingdom of Judah which only terminated in its meeting with a similar fate.

In the reign of Jehoiakim, in the year 599 b. c., Jerusalem was besieged and taken by Nebuchadnezzar, who carried away many of the people as captives to Babylon, and despoiled the temple of a large proportion of its treasures and sacred vessels.

In the reign of Jehoiachin, who succeeded his father Jehoiakim on the throne of Judah, Nebuchadnezzar again laid siege to Jerusalem. On its surrender, for it made but little resistance, Jehoiachin was carried to Babylon, where he remained a prisoner until his death. Nebuchadnezzar, on this invasion, took away ten thousand Jewish captives, consisting of all the remaining artificers and effective inhabitants, leaving behind only the poorer people

and the unskilled laborers. He also placed Zede
kiah, the uncle of Jehoiachin, upon the throne,
having first exacted from him an oath of fidelity and
allegiance.

The third and last invasion of Judah by Nebuchadnezzar was in the reign of this king, who
proved treacherous to his Babylonian master.
Nebuchadnezzar accordingly marched upon Jerusa
lem with a mighty army, and, having taken up his
own residence in Riblah, a town of Syria, he
dispatched Nebuzaradan, his general, or, as he is
called in Scripture. " captain of the guard," to the
city, which he took by storm after a twelve months'
siege.

On this occasion, the King of Chaldea was
resolved to inflict signal vengeance on his unfaith-
ful tributaries, and to leave no means for a renewed
revolt. He accordingly directed Nebuzaradan, after
having taken possession of all the vessels and
treasures of the temple which had escaped the
former pillage, and all the riches that he could find
in the king's house and the houses of the other inhabitants, to set fire to the temple and the city, and
completely to consume them ; to overthrow the walls,
the towers, and the fortresses, and in short to make
a thorough desolation of the place, in which condi
tion it remained for fifty two years, until there stora-
tion of the captives by Cyrus.

This is the calamitous event which is briefly referred to in a portion of the ceremonies of the Royal Arch, and which it is the sole object of the Super-Excellent Master's degree to commemorate.

ZEDEKIAH.

Zedekiah was the twentieth and last king of Judah. When Nebuchadnezzar had in his second siege of Jerusalem deposed Jehoiachin, whom he carried as a captive to Babylon, he placed Zedekiah on the throne in his stead. By this act Zedekiah became tributary to the King of the Chaldees, who exacted from him a solemn oath of fidelity and obedience. This oath he observed no longer than till an opportunity occurred of violating it. In the language of the author of the Books of Chronicles, " he rebelled against King Nebuchadnezzar, who had made him swear by God."

This course soon brought down upon him the vengeance of the offended monarch, who invaded the land of Judah with an immense army. Remaining himself at Riblah, a town on the northern border of Palestine, he sent the army under his general, Nebuzaradan, to Jerusalem, which was invested by the Babylonian forces. After a siege of about one year, during which the inhabitants endured many hardships, the city was taken by an assault the

Chaldeans entering it through breaches in the
northern wall.

It is very natural to suppose, that when the
enemy were most pressing in their attack upon the
devoted city, when the breach which was to give
them entrance had been effected, and when perhaps
the streets most distant from the temple were already
filled with Chaldean soldiery, a council of his princes
and nobles should have been held by Zedekiah
in the temple, to which they had fled for refuge, and
that he should ask their advice as to the most feasi-
ble method of escape from the impending dangers.
History, it is true, gives no account of any such
assembly, but the written record of these important
events which is now extant is very brief, and as
there is every reason to admit the probability of the
occurrence, the original compiler of the degree was
authorized to make the meeting of such a council
a part of its legendary ceremony. By the advice
of this council, Zedekiah attempted to make his
escape across the Jordan. The result is so suc-
cinctly told in the simple language of the prophet
Jeremiah, who was present during the siege and at
the capture, that no other words could give as good
a description.

" And it came to pass that when Zedekiah the
King of Judah saw them [the princes of Babylon]
and all the men of war, then they fled, and went

forth out of the city by night, by the way of the king's garden, by the gate betwixt the two walls: and he went out the way of the plain. But the Chaldeans' army pursued after them, and overtook Zedekiah in the plains of Jericho : and when they had taken him, they brought him up to Nebuchadnezzar king of Babylon to Riblah, in the land of Hamath, where he gave judgment upon him.

" Then the King of Babylon slew the sons of Zedekiah in Riblah before his eyes : also the King of Babylon slew all the nobles of Judah Moreover, he put out Zedekiah's eyes, and bound him with chains, to carry him to Babylon. And the Chaldeans burned the king's house and the houses of the people with fire, and brake down the walls of Jerusalem.

" Then Nebuzaradan, the Captain of the Guard, carried away captive into Babylon the remnant of the people that remained in the city, and those that fell away, that fell to him, with the rest of the people that remained. But Nebuzaradan, the Captain of the Guard, left of the poor of the people, which had nothing, in the land of Judah, and gave them vineyards and fields at the same time."*

Jeremiah, ch. xxxix. 4–10.

GEDALIAH.

There are five persons of the name of G ɪdaliah who are mentioned in Scripture, but only two of them were contemporary with the destruction of the temple.

Gedaliah the son of Pashur is mentioned by the prophet Jeremiah (xxxviii. 1) as a prince of the court of Zedekiah. He was present at its destruction, and is known to have been one of the advisers of the king. It was through his counsels, and those of his colleagues, that Zedekiah was persuaded to deliver up the prophet Jeremiah to death, from which he was rescued only by the intercession of a eunuch of the palace.

The other Gedaliah was the son of Ahikam. He seems to have been greatly in favor with Nebuchad-nezzar, for after the destruction of Jerusalem, and the deportation of Zedekiah, he was appointed by the Chaldean monarch as his satrap or governor over Judea. He took up his residence at Mizpah, where he was shortly afterwards murdered by Ish-mael, one of the descendants of the house of David.

The question now arises, which of these two is the one referred to in the ceremonies of a Council of Super-Excellent Masters? I think there can be to doubt that the founders of the degree intend I the second officer of the Council to represent the former, and not the latter; Gedaliah the son of Pashur, and not Gedaliah, the son of Ahikam; the Prince of Judah, and not the Governor of Judea.

We are forced to this conclusion by various reasons. The Gedaliah represented in the degree must have been a resident of Jerusalem during the siege, and at the very time of the assault, which immediately preceded the destruction of the temple and the city. Now, we know that Gedaliah the son of Pashur was with Hezekiah as one of his advisers. On the other hand it is most unlikely that Gedaliah the son of Ahikam could have been a resident of Jerusalem, for it is not at all probable that Nebuchadnezzar would have selected such an one for the important and confidential office of a satrap or governor. We should rather suppose that Gedaliah the son of Ahikam had been carried away to Babylon after one of the former sieges; that he had there, like Daniel, gained by his good conduct the esteem and respect of the Chaldean monarch; that he had come back to Judea with the army; and that, on the taking of the city, he had been appointed governor by Nebuchadnezzar. Such being the facts, it is evident that he could not have been in the council of King Zedekiah, advising and directing his attempted escape.

The modern revivers of the degree of Super

Excellent Master have, therefore, been wrong in supposing that Gedaliah the son of Ahikam, and afterwards Governor of Judea, was the person represented by the second officer of the Council. He was Gedaliah, the son of Pashur, a wicked man, one of Zedekiah's princes, and was most probably put to death by Nebuchadnezzar, with the other princes and nobles whom he captured in the plains of Jericho.

It may be said that it is not important to decide which Gedaliah is referred to, because the whole legend of the degree is apocryphal, not founded on history, but simply intended as an allegory or symbolic lesson.

To this I reply, that even in the composition of a fictitious work we should observe consistency, respect probabilities, and by all means avoid an absurdity.

CHARGE TO THE CANDIDATE.*

COMPANION:—As Masonry is a science of morality vailed in allegory and illustrated by

---

* This charge, which has never before been published, is, I think, the conclusion of Cushman's historical lecture on the degree. Its appropriateness has induced me to adopt it, with some slight variations of language, as the charge to the candidate; and as such it should be used. I am indebted for it to the kindness of Comp. Tho. Snow, of New Hampshire

symbols, it is proper that, as a Super Excellent Master, you should be instructed in the moral design of the degree into which you have just been initiated. It is intended, in the first place, to inculcate a sincere devotion to the GREAT I AM, in contradistinction to an idolatrous worship, which is, in other words, but a symbolical expression for a reverence of truth and an abhorrence of falsehood.

It also impresses on us the necessity of a faithful fulfillment of our several vows, and the fearless discharge of our respective duties; and teaches us, by its legends and its ceremonies, that the violation of our solemn vows, as in the instance of the last king of Judah, will not only cause us to forfeit the respect and friendship of our companions, but will also most surely destroy our own peace of mind.

Let us, then, labor diligently and faithfully in the cause of TRUTH, doing with all our might whatever our hands find to do, so that, when at the time of the third watch our work is finished, we may be greeted as Super-Excellent Masters, and be released from our captivity in the flesh, to return over the rough and rugged way of the Valley of the Shadow of Death to our abiding-place, eternal in the heavens, there to erect our second moral and Masonic temple, that house not made with hands, there to adore the Holy One of Israel throughout the endless circle of eternity.

Ceremonies of the Order.

CEREMONIES OF THE ORDER.

SECTION I.

CONSECRATION OF A NEW COUNCIL.

THE new Council will meet in its chamber, and open on the Select Master's degree. The Grand Officers will meet in an adjoining room, and on being notified by a Committee of the new Council that its members are ready for their reception, they will proceed to the Council Chamber, where, being received by the new Council with the usual honors, the officers of the new Council will resign their stations to the Grand Officers, and cause their jewels to be laid on the altar.

The ceremonies of Consecration will then commence, as follows : —

ANTHEM.

PRAYER.

Most holy and glorious Lord God, the Grand Architect of the Universe, thou who govern· est the world in the secrecy and silence of thy

5

omniscient counsels, and who showest mercy
unto all who trust in thy holy and ineffable
name; we invoke thy benediction upon the
purposes of our present assembly. May this
Council be established to thy honor, and consecrated to thy glory; may its officers be
endowed with wisdom to discern and fidelity
to pursue its true interests, and may its members, remembering that they have been chosen
as a select band to preserve for the Craft that
Divine Truth which is the Foundation Stone of
all Masonry, be ever mindful of the duty
which they owe to thee, the Eternal Builder,
the obedience they owe to their superiors, the
love they owe to their equals, and the good-will
they owe to all mankind.

Glory be to God on high.

Response. As it was in the beginning, is
now, and ever shall be, world without end.
So mote it be. *Amen.*

An appropriate Oration may then be delivered by
any Companion selected for the purpose.

The Grand Marshal will then form the new Council in front of the Most Puissant Grand Master.

The Illustrious Deputy Grand Master will then rise and say :—

Most Puissant Grand Master, a number of Companions, duly instructed in our sublime mysteries, being desirous of promoting the honor and propagating the principles of our Art, have applied to the Grand Council for a warrant to constitute a new Council of Royal and Select Masters, which having been obtained, they are now assembled for the purpose of being constituted and having their officers installed in due and ancient form.

MOST PUISSANT.—Let the Warrant of Constitution be read.

The GRAND RECORDER reads it.

MOST PUISSANT.—Companions, do you still approve of the officers as named herein ?

COMPANIONS.—We do.

Most PUISSANT.—By virtue of the powers in me vested, I do form you, my beloved Companions, into a Regular Council of Royal and Select Masters. Henceforth you are empowered and authorized to open and hold such a Council to initiate candidates therein, and to do and perform all such things as may there unto lawfully appertain; conforming in all your acts to the landmarks of the Order, and the Laws and Regulations of the Grand Council from which you have obtained your Warrant. And may the God of your fathers be with you, guide and direct you in all your doings.

Response. So mote it be. Amen.

The Stone of Foundation, represented by the Altar with the Substitute Ark upon it, having been previously covered with a linen cloth and placed in the center in front of the Most Puissant, is now uncovered, and the dedication proceeds.

The Grand Chaplain, with a pot of incense in his hand, says:

To our Most Excellent Grand Master, King Solomon, we solemnly dedicate this Council. May the blessing of Him who presides in the Grand Council above, descend and rest upon its members, and may their felicity be immortal. Glory be to God on high.

Response. As it was in the beginning, is now, and ever shall be, world without end Amen.

MUSIC.

The Deputy Grand Master then presents the Thrice Illustrious of the new Council to the Most Puissant, saying:

MOST PUISSANT GRAND MASTER! I present you Companion . . . ., nominated in the Warrant to be installed Thrice Illustrious of this new Council. I find him to be skilled in the Royal Mysteries, and zealous in diffusing the sacred principles of our fathers; and one in whose integrity and fidelity his Companions repose the highest confidence.

The Most Puissant then addresses him as follows:

THRICE ILLUSTRIOUS: I feel much satisfaction on the present occasion in installing you into the office of Thrice Illustrious Grand Master of this Council. It  is a station highly honorable to all those who diligently perform the important duties annexed to it. But before investing you with the appropriate insignia of your offices, I shall propose certain questions to you to which I must request your unequivocal answers.

1. Do you solemnly promise that you will use your utmost endeavors to correct the vices, purify the morals, and promote the happiness of your Companions?

2. That you will not suffer your Council to be opened unless there be nine Select Masters present?

3. That you will never permit more than twenty-seven Companions to take an active part in the initiation of any candidate into the mysteries of the Select degree?

4. That you will not suffer any person to pass the circle of perfection in your Council in whose integrity, fervency and, zeal you have not entire confidence?

5. That you will not acknowledge or hold intercourse with any Council that does not work under some regular and constitutional authority?

6. That you will admit no visitor into your Council who has not been regularly and lawfully invested with the degrees conferred therein until he has been formally healed?

7. That you will faithfully observe and maintain the By-laws of your Council, and the

Constitution and general regulations of the Grand Council under whose authority it is held?

8. That in the government of your Council you will administer justice tempered with mercy?

9. That you will pay due respect and obedience to the Grand Officers when duly installed, and sustain them in the discharge of their lawful duties?

Do you submit to all these charges, and do you promise to observe and practice them faithfully?

Response. I do.

MOST PUISSANT.—Your answers are satisfactory; but before proceeding further in your installation, it is necessary that I should administer to you the obligation of office.

The Most Puissant then administers the following obligation to the Thrice Illustrious :—

I, ..., do solemnly promise that I will serve this Council as Thrice Illustrious Grand Master for the time that I have been elected : that I will perform all the duties appertaining to that office to the best of my abilities, and will support and maintain the By-laws of my Council, and the Constitution of the Grand Council of . . . . .

The Most Puissant will then cause the Thrice Illustrious to be invested with the clothing and badges of his office, and address him as follows :—

Thrice Illustrious Grand Master; in consequence of your cheerful acquiescence with the charges which you have heard recited, and with entire confidence in the integrity of your character as a Select Master, you are now invested with the appropriate badges of your office.

Having been elevated by the voice of your Companions to the highest station in their gift, you are now to assume the functions of that office. It is your duty to set an example of diligence, industry, and fidelity; to see that the officers associated with you faithfully perform their respective duties; and that the interests and reputation of your Council are not endangered by imprudence or neglect The important trust committed to your charge will demand your earnest exertions for its faithful performance. As the representative of the wise king of Israel, it will be your duty to recite the secret traditions and illustrate the moral principles of the Order, to cherish the worthy, and hold in due veneration the ancient landmarks.

By a frequent recurrence to the by-laws of your Council, and the general regulations of the fraternity, together with a constant study of the legends and symbols of the Order, as explained in the history and lectures of the several degrees, you will be enabled to fulfill the important obligations resting upon you, with honor to yourself and advantage to the craft. And may He, without whose approbation all our labors are in vain, give wisdom to your counsels and strength to your exertions.

You will now take charge of your, officers standing on their right, and present them severally in succession to the Illustrious Deputy Grand Master, by whom they will be presented to me for installation.

The Thrice Illustrious will then present each of his officers in succession to the Illustrious Deputy

Grand Master, who will present the officers to the Most Puissant in the words already used in presenting the Thrice Illustrious, making the necessary variation of language to suit the office. The Most Puissant will then administer an obligation similar to that administered to the Thrice Illustrious, and after investing the officer with his clothing and badges, he will address him as follows :—

CHARGE TO ILLUSTRIOUS HIRAM OF TYRE.

 ILLUSTRIOUS COMPANION : You have been elected to the second office in this Council, and you are now invested with the appropriate badges of your office.

The duties of the important office to which your Companions have elevated you, will require your constant and earnest attention. You are to occupy the second seat in the Council; and it will be your duty to aid and support your Chief in all the requirements of his office. In his absence you are to preside, and to perform his duties.

Although the representative of a king, and therefore elevated in rank above your Com-

panions, you should never forget that in all
the duties which you owe to God, your neighbor, and yourself, you and they stand upon
the same level of equality. Let the bright
example of your illustrious predecessor in the
Grand Council at Jerusalem stimulate you to
the faithful performance of every duty; and
when the King of kings shall summon you
to His immediate presence, from His hand
may you receive a crown of glory which shall
never fade.

CHARGE TO THE PRINCIPAL CON-
DUCTOR OF THE WORKS.

COMPANION: As the third officer of this Council, you are invested with the appropriate
badges of your office. It is your
duty to sound the silver trump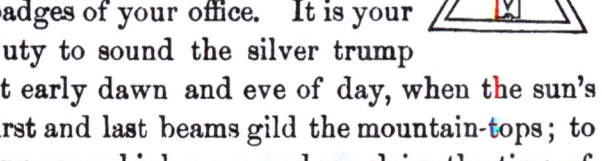
at early dawn and eve of day, when the sun's
first and last beams gild the mountain-tops; to
announce high noon, and proclaim the time of
labor and of rest.

In the absence of both your superior officers
you will be called upon to preside; and as the
interests of the Council should never be per-

mitted to suffer through a want of intelligence in its officers, you will allow me to urge upon you the necessity of being always prepared and qualified to meet such an emergency.

Having been admitted to the fellowship of kings, you will be appropriately reminded that the office of a mediator is one of great responsibility as well as honor. Let it therefore be your constant care to preserve harmony and unanimity of sentiment among the members of your Council. Discountenance whatever may tend to create division and dissension among the Companions in any of the departments of Masonry; and as the glorious sun, when at its meridian height, dispels the mist and clouds that obscure the horizon, so may your exertions tend to dissipate the mists of jealousy and discord, should they ever unfortunately arise in your Council.

CHARGE TO THE TREASURER.

COMPANION: You have been elected Treasurer of this Council, and I with pleasure invest you with the badge of your office. It is your duty to num-

ber and weigh out the shekels of the Sanc-
tuary, and to provide for the helpless orphan.
The qualities which should distinguish a
Treasurer are accuracy and fidelity: Accuracy
in keeping a fair and true account of the
receipts and disbursements; fidelity in carefully preserving the property and funds of the
Council, and in rendering a just account of
them when required. Your interest in this
Council, your attachment to the Craft, and
your known integrity of character, are a suffi-
cient guaranty that the duties of your office
will be faithfully performed.

CHARGE TO THE RECORDER.

COMPANION: You have been
elected Recorder of this Council,
and I with pleasure invest you
with the badge of your office.
It is your duty to keep a fair

record of all things proper to be written; to
receive all moneys, and pay them over to the
Treasurer. The qualities, therefore, which
should recommend a Recorder are correctness
in recording the proceedings of the Council;

judgment in discriminating between what is
proper and what is improper to be written;
regularity in making the returns to the
Grand Council; integrity in accounting for all
moneys that pass through his hands; and
fidelity in paying the same over to the Treasurer. The possession of these qualities has
designated you as a suitable Companion for
this office; and I do not doubt that you will
discharge its duties with fidelity and diligence. And when you shall have completed
the record of your transactions here below,
and finished the term of your probation, may
you be admitted into the Grand Council
above, and find your name recorded in the
book of life eternal.

CHARGE TO THE CAPTAIN OF THE GUARDS.

COMPANION : Having been elected Captain of the Guards, I present you with the badge and
appropriate implement of your
office.   Guard well your post,
and suffer none to pass it but the select, the

worthy, and the faithful. Be ever attentive to the commands of your chief, and be always near at hand to see them duly executed.

CHARGE TO THE CONDUCTOR OF THE COUNCIL.

COMPANION: You have been elected Conductor of the Council, and I invest you with the badge of your office. It is your duty to attend to the preparation of candidates, and to see that the Council is duly guarded. In the discharge of the duties which you have assumed, be fervent and zealous; let uprightness and integrity attend your steps; and let justice and mercy mark your conduct.

CHARGE TO THE STEWARD.

COMPANION: You have been appointed Steward of this Council, and I now invest you with the badge and implement of your office. The duties of a Steward in a Select Council are in general the same as those which devolve on a Tiler in a lodge of Ancient Craft Masonry; and as you are furnished with a sword to enable you to guard the Council Chamber and the entrance to the secret passage against intruders, so should it symbolically serve as a constant admonition to us, to set a guard at the entrance of our thoughts; to place a watch at the door of our lips; to post a sentinel at the avenue of our actions, thereby excluding every unworthy thought, word, and deed, and enabling us to preserve our consciences void of offense toward God and man.

CHARGE TO THE MEMBERS OF THE COUNCIL.

COMPANIONS: From the nature of the constitution of every society, some must rule and others obey. And while justice and moderation are required of the officers in the discharge of their official duties, subordination and respect for their rulers are equally demanded of the members. The relation is reciprocal. The interests of both are inseparable; and without mutual co-operation, the labors of neither can succeed. A house divided against itself cannot stand. Let therefore brotherly love prevail among you; let each be emulous of the others in all good works; in promoting peace and unity; and in striving to see who best can rule and best obey. Let the avenues to your passions be strictly guarded; let no curious intruder find his way into the secret recesses of your retirement, to disturb the harmony which should ever prevail among the select and chosen, and mar the respect of your Companions and the commendation of your own consciences.

The officers and members of the Council will then pass in review in front of the Grand Officers, with their hands crossed on their breasts, bowing as they pass.

The Grand Marshal then makes the following proclamation:

"In the name of the Most Puissant Grand Council of the State of . . . . . . I hereby proclaim . . . . Council Number . . . to be legally constituted and consecrated, and the officers thereof duly installed with the Grand Honors of Masonry, by three times three."

The Grand Honors * are then given.

The following or some other appropriate **Ode or Anthem** should be sung :—

ODE.

Now the work is completed and all are combined,
    To close in the secret and deep-hidden cell
The words which are treasured as light to the mind,
    Like the waters of truth in their close-covered well.
Here, safely secured, they shall live in the rock,
    When the storm rages o'er it and levels the wall,
And still in the rage of the *conqueror's* shock,
    The arches shall neither be shaken nor fall.

We have laid in its secret and silent retreat
    The treasures that kings shall exult to behold;
And the *pilgrim* shall hasten with ardor to meet
    This gift, valued higher than jewels or gold:

---

* As the Royal and Select degrees were originally derived from the Ancient and Accepted Rite, it is to be presumed that the honors or battery of that rite must on such occasions have been originally practiced. But their present position, and their history, which connects them with the first temple, make it proper that now the honors of Ancient Craft Masonry should be used.

Ages roll on their way and no foot shall be heard
　　In search of this roll to enlighten the world;
But a hand shall be found to recover the *Word*,
　　And then shall the standard of *truth* be unfurled.

Benediction by the Grand Chaplain.

The Grand Officers will then retire, and the Council wil be closed by its own officers.

SECTION II.

On the night appointed for the installation, the
Council being opened in the Select Degree, a Past
Thrice Illustrious, either of that or some other
Council, will take the chair and another Past
Thrice Illustrious or some other officer will present
the Thrice Illustrious elect to the Presiding Officer
and say :

THRICE ILLUSTRIOUS : I present before you
Companion   . . .   who has been duly
elected to serve this Council, as its Thrice
Illustrious Grand Master for the ensuing masonic year, and who now declares himself ready
for installation.

The Presiding Officer then addresses him as follows :

THRICE ILLUSTRIOUS : I feel much satisfaction
on the present occasion, in installing you into
the office of **Thrice Illustrious Grand Master** of

this Council. It is a station highly honorable to all those who diligently perform the important duties annexed to it. But before investing you with the appropriate insignia of your office, I shall propose certain questions, to which I must request your unequivocal answers.

1. Do you solemnly promise that you will use your utmost endeavors to correct the vices, purify the morals, and promote the happiness of your Companions ?

2. That you will not suffer your Council to be opened unless there be nine Select Masters present ?

3. That you will never permit more than twenty-seven Companions to take an active part in the initiation of any candidate into the mysteries of the Select Degree ?

4. That you will not suffer any person to pass the circle of perfection in your Council in whose integrity, fervency, and zeal you have not entire confidence ?

5. That you will not acknowledge or hold intercourse with any Council that does not

work under some regular and constitutional authority?

6. That you will admit no visitor into your Council, who has not been regularly and lawfully invested with the degrees conferred therein, until he has been formally healed?

7. That you will faithfully observe and maintain the By-laws of your Council and the Constitution, and General Regulations of the Grand Council, under whose authority it is held?

8. That in the government of your Council you will administer justice tempered with mercy?

9. That you will pay due respect and obedience to the Grand Officers when duly installed, and sustain them in the discharge of their lawful duties?

Do you submit to all these charges, and do you promise to observe them faithfully?

Response. I do.

PRESIDING OFFICER.—Your answers are satisfactory; but before proceeding further in your installation, it is necessary that I should administer to you the obligation of office.

The Presiding Officer then administers the following obligation to the Thrice Illustrious elect:—

I . . . . do solemnly promise that I will serve this Council as Thrice Illustrious Grand Master for the time that I have been elected; that I will perform all the duties appertaining to that office to the best of my abilities, and will support and maintain the By-laws of my Council and the Constitution of the Grand Council of . . .

The Presiding Officer will then cause the Thrice Illustrious elect to be invested with the badges of his office, and addresses him as follows:

 THRICE ILLUSTRIOUS GRAND MASTER: In consequence of your cheerful acquiescence with the charges which you have heard recited, and with entire confidence in the integrity of your character, as a Select Master, you are now invested with the appropriate badges of your office.

Having been elevated by the voice of your

Companions to the highest station in their gift, you are now to assume the functions of that office. It is your duty to set an example of diligence, industry, and fidelity; to see that the officers associated with you faithfully perform their respective duties; and that the interests and reputation of your Council are not endangered by imprudence or neglect. The important trust committed to your charge will demand your earnest exertions for its faithful performance. As the representative of the wise king of Israel, it will be your duty to recite the secret traditions and illustrate the moral principles of the Order, to cherish the worthy and hold in due veneration the ancient landmarks.

By a frequent recurrence to the By-laws of your Council, and the general regulations of the fraternity, together with a constant study of the legends and symbols of the Order, as explained in the history and lectures of the several degrees, you will be enabled to fulfill the important obligations resting upon you with honor to yourself and advantage to the craft. And may He, without whose approbation all our labors are in vain, give wisdom to your counsels and strength to your exertions.

The Presiding Officer then inducts the newly installed Thrice Illustrious into his chair, who, for the remainder of the ceremony, acts. as the installing officer. Each of the subordinate officers is presented to him, with the same formula that is recited above. The same obligation (with the necessary variation of title) which had been taken by the Thrice Illustrious is administered, and the charge read to each of the officers by the Thrice Illustrious elect, after which the newly installed officer takes his appropriate station in the Council.

CHARGE TO ILLUSTRIOUS HIRAM OF TYRE.

ILLUSTRIOUS COMPANION: You have been elected to the second office in this Council, and you are now invested with the appropriate badges of your office.

The duties of the important office to which your Companions have elevated you will require your constant and earnest attention. You are to occupy the second seat in the Council; and it will be your duty to aid and

6

support your chief in all the requirements of his office. In his absence you are to preside and perform his duties.

Although the representative of a king, and therefore elevated in rank above your Companions, you should never forget that in all the duties which you owe to God, your neighbor, and yourself, you and they stand upon the same level of equality. Let the bright example of your illustrious predecessor in the Grand Council at Jerusalem stimulate you to the faithful performance of every duty; and when the King of kings shall summon you to His immediate presence, from His hand may you receive a crown of glory which shall never fade.

CHARGE TO THE PRINCIPAL CONDUCTOR OF THE WORKS.

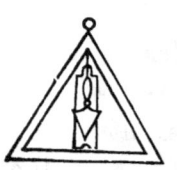

COMPANION: As the third offi cer of this Council you are in- vested with the appropriate badges of your office. It is your duty to sound the silver trump at early dawn and eve of day, when the sun's first and last beams gild the mountain-tops, to announce high noon and proclaim the time of labor and of rest.

In the absence of both your superior officers, you will be called upon to preside ; and, as the interests of the Council should never be permitted to suffer through a want of intelligence in its officers, you will allow me to urge upon you the necessity of being always prepared and qualified to meet such an emergency.

Having been admitted to the fellowship of kings, you will be appropriately reminded that the office of a mediator is one of great responsibility as well as honor. Let it therefore be your constant care to preserve harmony and unanimity of sentiment among the members of your Council. Discountenance whatever may tend to create division and dissension among the Companions in any of the departments of Masonry ; and as the glorious sun, when at its meridian height, dispels the mists and clouds that obscure the horizon, so may your exertions tend to dissipate the mists of jealousy and discord, should they ever unfortunately arise in your Council.

CHARGE TO THE TREASURER.

 COMPANION: You have been elected Treasurer of this Council, and I with pleasure invest you with the badge of your office. It is your duty to number and weigh out the shekels of the Sanctuary, and to provide for the helpless orphan. The qualities which should distinguish a Treasurer are accuracy and fidelity. Accuracy in keeping a fair and true account of the receipts and disbursements; fidelity in carefully preserving the property and funds of the Council, and in rendering a just account of them when required. Your interest in this Council, your attachment to the Craft, and your known integrity of character, are a sufficient guaranty that the duties of your office will be faithfully performed.

CHARGE TO THE RECORDER.

COMPANION: You have been elected Recorder of this Council, and I with pleasure invest you with the badge of your office. It is your duty to keep a fair  record of all things proper to be written, to receive all moneys and pay them over to the Treasurer. The qualities, therefore, which should recommend a Recorder are correctness in recording the proceedings of the Council; judgment in discriminating between what is proper and what is improper to be written; regularity in making the returns to the Grand Council; integrity in accounting for all moneys that pass through his hands; and fidelity in paying the same over to the Treasurer. The possession of these qualities has designated you as a suitable Companion for this office; and I do not doubt that you will discharge its duties with fidelity and diligence. And when you shall have completed the record of your transactions here below, and finished the term of your probation, may you be admitted into the Grand Council above, and find your name recorded in the book of life eternal.

CHARGE TO THE CAPTAIN OF THE GUARDS.

COMPANION : Having been elected Captain of the Guards, I present you with the badge and appropriate implement of your office. Guard well your post, and suffer none to pass it but the select, the worthy, and the faithful. Be ever attentive to the commands of your chief, and be always near at hand to see them duly executed.

CHARGE TO THE CONDUCTOR OF THE COUNCIL.

COMPANION : You have been elected Conductor of the Council, and I invest you with the badge of your office. It is your duty to attend to the preparation of candidates and to see that the Council is duly guarded. In the discharge of the duties which you have assumed, be fervent and zealous; let uprightness and integrity attend your steps; and let justice and mercy mark your conduct.

CHARGE TO THE STEWARD.

COMPANION: You have been appointed Steward of this Council, and I now invest you with the badge and implement of your office. The duties of a 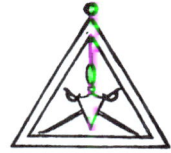 Steward in a Select Council are in general the same as those which devolve on a Tiler in a lodge of Ancient Craft Masonry; and as you are furnished with a sword to enable you to guard the Council Chamber and the entrance to the secret passage against intruders, so should it symbolically serve as a constant admonition to us, to set a guard at the entrance of our thoughts; to place a watch at the door of our lips; to post a sentinel at the avenue of our actions, thereby excluding every unworthy thought, word, and deed, and enabling us to preserve our consciences void of offense toward God and man.

CHARGE TO THE MEMBERS OF THE COUNCIL.

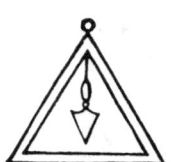

COMPANIONS: From the nature of the constitution of every society, some must rule and others obey. And while justice and moderation are required of the officers in the discharge of their official duties, subordination and respect for their rulers are equally demanded of the members. The relation is reciprocal. The interests of both are inseparable; and without mutual co-operation, the labors of neither can succeed. A house divided against itself cannot stand. Let, therefore, brotherly love prevail among you; let each be emulous of the others in all good works; in promoting peace and unity; and in striving to see who best can rule and best obey. Let the avenues to your passions be strictly guarded; let no curious intruder find his way into the secret recesses of your retirement, to disturb the harmony which should ever prevail among the select and chosen, and mar the respect of your Compan-

ions and the commendation of your own consciences.

The Presiding Officer who had installed the Thrice
Illustrious elect, then makes the following proclamation:

" In the name of the Most Puissant Grand
Council of the State of . . . . I hereby proclaim the Officers of . . . . . . Council No. . . to
be duly installed, with the Grand Honors of
Masonry, by three times three.

The Grand Honors are then given, and the ceremony of installation is concluded.

SECTION III.

At the time appointed for the Installation, the Grand Council being opened in the Select Master's degree, the chair must be taken by a Past Most Puissant, or, if none be present, by some officer who is, or has been, the Thrice Illustrious of a Council.

The highest Grand or Past Grand Officer present then introduces the Most Puissant Grand Master elect, divested of the robes and jewels of his office, to the installing officer, saying:

Most Puissant: I present before you Companion . . . . . . , who having been duly elected Most Puissant Grand Master of the Grand Council of . . . . . , now declares himself ready for installation.

The Presiding Officer then directs him to approach, and administers to him the following obligation, all the Companions standing:

6*

I . . . . . . do solemnly promise that I will serve as Most Puissant Grand Master of the Grand Council of . . . . . for the term for which I have been elected, and will perform all the duties appertaining to that office to the best of my abilities, and will support and maintain the Constitution of the Grand Council of . . . . So help me God.

The Installing Officer will then invest the Most Puissant elect with the insignia of his office, after which he will deliver to him the following

CHARGE.

MOST PUISSANT: By the voice of your Companions you have been chosen to occupy the most important and the most honorable office in their power to bestow, and to me has been intrusted the pleasing duty of investing you with its insignia.

You have been too long a member of our ancient Craft to require, now, any instructions in relation to the duties of your office. I do not doubt that you will be constant and regular in your attendance on the convocations of the Grand Council; watching with fidelity and judgment the conduct of the subordinate bodies within your jurisdiction; and while tempering justice with mercy, will require from every member a due obedience to the rules and regulations of our Institution.

Especially is it your province to hold in veneration the ancient landmarks of the Order. It therefore becomes your most sacred duty, to see that, during your administration, not the least of them may be removed. May He, without whose approbation all our labors are in vain, give strength to your endeavors and support your exertions.

You will now assume your appropriate station, and instruct your subordinates in the duties which they are respectively required to discharge.

After he has taken his seat in the chair, the Grand Marshal will make proclamation as follows :

In the name of the Grand Council of . . . . . I do hereby proclaim that Companion . . . . . . has been duly installed as Most Puissant Grand

Master, with the Grand Honors of Masonry, by three times three.

The Grand Honors are then given.

Each of the other Officers is then presented in the same manner to the new Most Puissant, who, after administering a similar obligation, with the necessary change of title, delivers the charge. The Officer, as soon as he has been installed, will assume his appropriate station in the Grand Council.

CHARGE TO THE THRICE ILLUSTRIOUS DEPUTY GRAND MASTER.

THRICE ILLUSTRIOUS COMPANION : The important station to which you have been elected requires from you exemplary conduct, and its duties demand your most assiduous attention.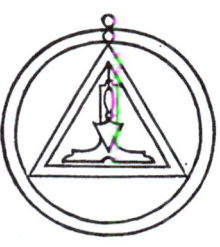

In the absence of the Most Puissant you are to preside ; in his presence you are to strengthen and support his authority by your counsel and advice.

Let the bright example of the illustrious monarch of Tyre, who, by his power and wealth, gave strength to the labors of King Solomon, stimulate you to the faithful discharge of your duties; and when the King of kings shall summon you to His immediate presence, from His hand may you receive a crown of glory that shall never fade.

CHARGE TO THE ILLUSTRIOUS GRAND CONDUCTOR OF THE WORKS.

ILLUSTRIOUS COMPANION: The office to which you have been elected is one of great importance. In the absence of your superior officers it is your prerogative to succeed them and to perform their duties. The purposes of the Institution should never suffer for want of intelligence in its proper officers. You will therefore perceive the necessity there is of youi possessing such qualifications as will enable you to accomplish those duties which are incumbent upon you in your appropriate station, as well as those which may occasionally devolve upon you by the absence of your superiors.

Remember the example of that illustrious artist at Jerusalem, who was ever ready, as a mediator, to cause justice to be tempered with mercy, and to preserve peace and order among the Craft. Let it remind you that the harmony and unanimity of the Order should be your constant aim. And as the glorious sun at its meridian height dispels the mists and clouds which obscure the horizon, so may your exertions tend to dissipate the clouds of jealousy and discord whensoever they may appear.

CHARGE TO THE GRAND TREASURER.

ILLUSTRIOUS COMPANION: You have been elected to the responsible office of Grand Treasurer, and I now invest you with the badge of your office.

It is your duty to receive all moneys due the Grand Council from the hands of the Grand Recorder: make due entries of the same, and pay them out by order of the Most Puissant, and with the consent and approbation of the

Grand Council. The office to which you have been elected embraces an important trust, and the choice of you by your Companions is an evidence of the high opinion they entertain of your fidelity and discretion.

CHARGE TO THE GRAND RECORDER.

 ILLUSTRIOUS COMPANION: You have been elected to the important office of Grand Recorder, and I now invest you with the jewel of your office.

It is your duty to receive all moneys due the Grand Council, and pay them over to the Grand Treasurer, taking his receipt for the same; to observe all the proceedings of the Grand Council, and to make a true record of all things proper to be written. You are also the official organ of the Grand Council, and in that capacity will conduct its various correspondence and act as the medium of intercourse between the fraternity and their presiding Officer. In the discharge of these extensive duties, let your carriage and behavior be marked with that promptitude and discretion that will at once reflect credit on yourself, and honor on the body whom you represent.

CHARGE TO THE GRAND CHAPLAIN.

ILLUSTRIOUS COMPANION
The sacred position of Grand Chaplain has been intrusted to your care, and I now invest you with the jewel of your office.

In the discharge of your duties you will be required to lead the devotional exercises of our Grand Convocations, and to perform the sacred functions of your holy calling at our public ceremonies. Though Masonry be not religion, it is emphatically religion's handmaid, and hence, in ministering at its altar, the services you may perform will lose nothing of their vital influences, because they are practiced in that spirit of universal tolerance which distinguishes our Institution. The doctrines of morality and virtue, which you are accustomed to inculcate to the world, will form the appropriate lessons which you are expected to communicate to your Companions. I do not doubt that you will discharge the duties of your present appointment with steadfastness and energy in well doing.

CHARGE TO THE GRAND MARSHAL.

ILLUSTRIOUS COMPANION : You have been elected Grand Marshal, and I now invest you with the jewel of your office, and present you with this baton, as the ensign of your authority.

It is your duty to proclaim the Grand Officers at their installation; to arrange all processions of the Grand Council, and to preserve order according to the forms prescribed. Skill and precision are essentially necessary to the faithful discharge of these duties.

CHARGE TO THE GRAND CAPTAIN OF THE GUARDS.

ILLUSTRIOUS COMPANION:
You have been elected Grand
Captain of the Guards, and I
invest you with the jewel of
your office. Guard well your
post, and suffer none to pass
it but the select, the faithful, and the worthy.
Be ever attentive to the commands of your
Chief, and always near at hand to see them
duly executed. I present you with this sword
as the appropriate implement of your office.

CHARGE TO THE GRAND CONDUCTOR OF THE COUNCIL.

ILLUSTRIOUS COMPANION:
You have been elected Grand
Conductor of the Council, and
I invest you with the jewel
of your office. Your duties
are not the less important
because they are subordinate in their character.

In their discharge you, station is near the door, whence you will receive all reports from the Grand Steward, and announce the name and Masonic rank of all who desire admission. You will see that none enter without wearing their appropriate decorations. I present you with this rod as the badge of your authority.

CHARGE TO THE GRAND STEWARD.

 COMPANION: You have been appointed Grand Steward, and I now invest you with the jewel of your office, and place this sword in your hands, the more effectually to enable you to repel the approach of intruders, and to guard against surprise.

It is your duty to guard the door of the Grand Council on the outside; to report to the Grand Conductor those who desire to be admitted; to place the Council Chamber in order for convocations; and to attend to such other duties as may be required of you by the Grand Council. Your early and punctual attention is essentially necessary.

The Grand Marshal then makes proclamation as follows:

By authority of the Grand Council of . . . . I proclaim that the Grand Officers have been installed in ample form, with the Grand Honors of Masonry, by three times three.

The Grand Honors are then given, and the ceremony of installation is concluded.

CONSTITUTIONAL RULES

FOUNDED ON THE ANCIENT LANDMARKS AND USAGES
OF CRYPTIC MASONRY.

1. WHEN the Most Puissant is absent from the Grand Council, the chair shall be taken by the Deputy Grand Master. If both are absent, the Grand Principal Conductor of the Works must take the chair. If all these officers are absent, the Senior Past Grand Officer, not less in dignity than a Past Grand Principal Conductor of the Works, must preside. If no such Past Grand Officer be present, the duty of presiding will devolve on the Thrice Illustrious of the oldest Council present.

2. When the Thrice Illustrious of a subordinate Council is absent, his duties must be performed by the Illustrious H. of T. ; if both be absent, by the Principal Conductor of the Works. If he likewise be absent, the chair must be taken by a Past Thrice Illustrious of the Council. But if no such officer be present, the Council cannot be opened. The Warrant of Constitution is granted to the Thrice Illustrious Grand Master, the Illustrious Hiram of Tyre,

and the Principal Conductor of the Works, and to their successors in office, and to none else; and none else can lawfully act.

3. No officer of a Grand or Subordinate Council can be recognized as such, until he has been installed.

4. Every officer holds on to his office until his successor has been installed.

5. No officer can resign his office after he has been installed. Nor can any election be held, except at the constitutional convocation for that purpose, unless by dispensation.

6. No Council can, at an extra convocation, alter or expunge the proceedings of a regular one.

7. No Council can interfere in the business of another Council, or give the degrees to candidates who have been accepted by other Councils, without their consent.

8. The degrees of Royal and Select Master, when conferred in a chapter of Royal Arch Masons, are illegal and irregular, and no Council can recognize persons who have so received the degrees. Nor can any Royal or Select Master sit in a chapter while these degrees are being thus irregularly conferred.

9. The degrees of Royal and Select Master can only be conferred on worthy Royal Arch Masons.

10. No candidate can receive the Council degrees who is deformed, maimed, or imperfect in his limbs.

11. No candidate can be elected to receive the degrees, nor Select Master affiliated in any Council, without the unanimous consent of all the members present.

12. All ballotings for candidates and trials of Companions must take place in the Select Master's degree. But a Royal Master may be tried in the Royal Master's degree, yet the final vote shall be taken in a Council of Select Masters.

13. None but Select Masters can be permitted to make any motion, vote, or join in any debate.

14. Every subordinate Council, as well as every member of the same, has the right of appeal to the Grand Council, whose decision shall be final.

15. Every Council must meet at least once in every three months, and no Council can suspend its convocations unless by dispensation from the Grand Council or presiding Grand Officer.

16. No Council of Royal Masters can be opened unless there be five Royal Masters present.

17. No Council of Select Masters can be opened unless there be nine Select Masters present.

18. In conferring the Select degree, not more than twenty-seven Select Masters should be present. If

there be more, they are to be constructively considered as absent, and must take no part in the work.

19. Although the use of the vails of a chapter in working the Select degree is usual and convenient, it should be discountenanced as irregular, and destructive of the symbolism of the degree. No Select Council should work with less than the required number of nine arches.

20. No Council can be opened or holden except by the authority of a warrant of Constitution granted by a Grand Council or a dispensation issued by a Most Puissant Grand Master.

21. No Council in one State, where there is a Grand Council, can work under a warrant granted by the Grand Council of another State.

22. No warrant or dispensation for the opening of a new Council can be granted except upon the petition of nine Select Masters.

23. The election of officers in a subordinate Council must be holden at the stated convocation, which is at the meeting next preceding the Festival of St. John the Evangelist, and the installation must take place as soon after the election as possible. Where, from any cause, the election has not been holden at the stated period, a dispensation from the Most Puissant will be required for holding at it any subsequent period.

7

24. No Council can suspend its By-laws.

25. There can be no appeal from the decision of the Presiding Officer of a Council to the Council. The Grand Council can alone reverse such decision.

26. It is requisite that at least three subordinate Councils should unite to form and constitute a Grand Council in any State or Territory. And when a Grand Council has been so formed, it becomes the supreme authority as to Cryptic Masonry in that State or Territory.

27. All documents relating to Cryptic Masonry must be dated from the last year of the building of King Solomon's Temple, at which time the Royal and Select Degrees are supposed by their legend to have been instituted. The temple was completed in the year of the world 3000, or 1000 years before the birth of Christ, and the number 1000 must therefore be added to the current year to obtain the true date. In reference to that sacred deposit, which it was the object of the Select Degree to preserve, this date is characterized as *Anno Depositionis*, or *in the Year of the Deposit*. Thus the year of the common era, 1870, should, in a document of Cryptic Masonry, be designated as Anno Depositionis, or in the Year of the Deposit, 2870.

ESTABLISHMENT OF THE COUNCIL DEGREES IN AMERICA.

FORTY years ago there were very earnest discussions on the subject of the origin and jurisdiction of the degrees of Royal and Select Master. At that time there were three authorities under whom those degrees were conferred in the United States: first, under Grand Councils in some of the States; secondly, under Grand Chapters, as in Maryland and Virginia; and thirdly, under the Supreme Council of the thirty-third degree of the Ancient and Accepted Rite, as in South Carolina. This diversity of authority was undoubtedly dependent on an uncertainty of origin. The degrees were here, but few knew whence they came, nor by whom they had been originally introduced.

But an attempt on the part of the Grand Chapter of Maryland, in the year 1826, "to assume jurisdiction and authority" over these degrees, led to investigations into their history. In February, 1827, a

committee of most able and competent Companions
made a report on this subject to the Grand Chapter
of South Carolina, in which the history of the origin
of these degrees is so fully discussed, that the valuable information it imparts had better be given in
the very words of the report itself:

"The committee appointed at the last stated convocation of the Grand Royal Arch Chapter, in May
last, to take into consideration and report upon the
propriety and expediency of the different Grand
Royal Arch Chapters of the several States respectively assuming jurisdiction and authority over the
Royal and Select Master's degrees, and to which
committee were referred the proceedings of the
Grand Royal Arch Chapter of Maryland upon the
subject, respectfully ask leave to state, that they
have made extensive and careful investigation into
the subjects referred to their consideration, and they
offer the following statement as the result of their
inquiries:

"They have ascertained that the respectable brothers and companions, Dr. F. Dalcho, Dr. Isaac Auld,
Dr. James Moultrie, Sr., and Moses C. Levy, Esq.,
with many others, received these degrees in Charleston, in February, 1783, in the Sublime Grand Lodge
of Perfection, then established in this city (Charleston), of which body three of the above-named brothers are still living, venerable for their years and

warm attachment to the glorious cause of Freemasonry, and highly respected and esteemed in the community where they have so long and so honorably sojourned, and they are still members of the same sublime body.

"Your committee have further ascertained that at the original establishment of the Grand Council of Princes of Jerusalem, in this city, on the 20th of February, 1783, by the Illustrious Brothers Joseph Myers, Barend M. Spitzer, and A. Forst, Deputy Inspectors-General, from Frederick II., King of Prussia, Brother Myers then deposited in the archives of the said Grand Council of the Princes of Jerusalem certified copies of the said degrees, from Berlin, in Prussia, which were to be under the future guidance and fostering protection of the government of the above-named presiding body. The above-named three respectable brethren and companions are, and have steadily been, members and officers of the said body of Princes of Jerusalem; their evidence therefore must be conclusive upon these points.

"Your committee are informed that the above-named Brother Myers, previously to his return to Europe, while pursuing his mercantile concerns, resided some time in several of the cities of Virginia and Maryland, where he communicated a knowledge of the degrees in question.

" The committee further state, that the Grand Officers and the Sublime Council of Inspectors-General have been, since 1783, steadily in the habit of conferring the degrees in question, under their authority, in the Southern and Western States. Your committee have seen and perused the first copy of these degrees that ever came to America, and old copies of Charters that have been returned by Councils in States where Grand Councils have been formed, and the bodies surrendering have taken other Charters for conferring the degrees from such Grand Councils of Royal and Select Masters thus formed.

" From these statements the Grand Royal Arch Chapter will readily perceive that these degrees have been under a regular and independent Masonic protection and authority for more than forty-six years, and that they were thus circumstanced in the United States of America at a period long antecedent to the establishment of Grand Royal Arch Chapters, or even of Chapters of Royal Arch Masons, in any part of the world."

As corroborative of these statements, it may be mentioned that in a manuscript record of Brother Peter Snell, who was, in 1827, a member of the Supreme Council, is contained the following memorandum :

" Supreme Council Chamber, Charleston, S. C.,

February 10, 1827. I hereby certify that the detached degrees, called Royal and Select Master, or Select Masters of 27, were regularly given by the Sublime Grand Lodge of Perfection (No. 2, in the U. S. A.), established by Brother Isaac Da Costa, in Charleston, in February, 1783, one of the original members of which, M. I. Brother Moses C. Levy, is still alive and a member of it to this day, without ceasing to be so for a day. And further, that at the first establishment of a Grand Council of Princes of Jerusalem, in Charleston, in February, 1783, by the Illustrious Deputy Inspectors-General, Joseph Myers, B. M. Spitzer, and A. Forst, Brother Myers (who succeeded Brother Da Costa, after his decease) deposited a certified copy of the degrees from Berlin, in Prussia, to be under the guidance and fostering protection of the government of the above Grand Council of Princes of Jerusalem."

Brother Moses Holbrook, who was Grand Commander of the Supreme Council at Charleston in 1829, has copied this statement of Snell into a manuscript ritual of the degrees, which he deposited in the archives of the Supreme Council, and which is now in the possession of a Past Officer. He has also added in his own hand the following comment:

" Brother Myers, shortly after this (February 20, 1788), resided some time in Norfolk, Richmond, and Baltimore, previous to his removal to Europe, and he communicated a knowledge of these degrees to a number of brethren in those cities. The original copy is still in my keeping; and agreeably to the obligations of the same, and the Grand Constitutions governing those degrees, viz.: Royal and Select Masters of 27, it is correct and lawful to give them either to Sublime Masons, who have arrived to the Knights of the Ninth Arch (13th degree), or to Companions of the Third Arch, Royal Arch Masons."

Finally, the Rev. Frederick Dalcho, who was at one time Grand Commander of the Southern Supreme Council, in the appendix to his "Masonic Orations," published in 1803, after giving a list of the regular degrees of the Ancient and Accepted Rite, adds, that "most of the Inspectors are in possession of a number of detached degrees given in different parts of the world, and which they generally communicate, free of expense, to those brethren who are high enough to understand them." And among these "detached degrees," he mentions "Select Masons of 27," which is what we now call the Select Master.

From these statements, then, we gather the following results as to the history of the introduction of these degrees into the United States.

1. The degrees of Royal and Select Master were originally brought to this country by an Inspector-General of the Ancient and Accepted Rite, in the

year 1783, deposited by him in the archives, and placed under the control of the Council of Princes of Jerusalem, which was organized in the city of Charleston, South Carolina, in that year.

2. These degrees were at first conferred in Charleston, by the Council of Princes of Jerusalem, as "detached degrees," or what in more modern phrase would be called "side degrees" of the Ancient and Accepted Rite.

3. They were disseminated over the whole country by agents or representatives of this Rite, who conferred them on any qualified persons whom they pleased to select, but always with the administration of a pledge of allegiance to the Supreme Council of the Ancient and Accepted Rite.

4. Charters were granted by these agents of the Supreme Council for the establishment of Councils of Royal and Select Masters, in different States, which Councils subsequently united in the formation of State Grand Councils, and threw off their allegiance to the Supreme Council of the A. and A. Rite. I do not believe that charters were ever granted immediately and directly by the Supreme Council. I think that they were always issued in its name by its agents, who were empowered so to do by a general warrant. Thus I have been enabled to trace the original Councils of Alabama to the action of John Barker, who was an authorized agent of the Supreme

7*

Council. Perhaps more work was done in this way by Jeremy L. Cross, under the same claim, than by any other man in the United States.

In this manner the control of these degrees has been gradually but permanently taken from the Supreme Council of the Ancient and Accepted Rite, and they have now become a constituent part of what is beginning to be called the American Rite, to which, indeed, they properly belong, since they are absolutely necessary for the proper illustration of the Royal Arch degree.

The Inspectors-General of the Ancient and Accepted Rite, at least in the Southern Council, still claim, although they very seldom exercise it, the right to confer these degrees on qualified persons, and it can hardly be denied that Royal and Select Masters, so made, would be legal and regular. To doubt it would be to throw suspicion on the legality of every Council and every Select Master of the present day, since they derive their existence from founders originally made in this way by Inspectors-General. If the fountain is defiled, we can hardly expect that the streams which flow from it should be pure.

This connection of the degrees of Royal and Select Master with the Ancient and Accepted Rite, will readily account for tne resemblance which is found in these degrees, in phraseo.ogy and symbolism, to that Rite. Their legends, however, assimilate them more closely to the Royal Arch of the York and American Rites, than to the corresponding Knights of the Ninth Arch of the Ancient and Accepted Rite. Hence, in making them the eighth and ninth degrees of the American Rite, it must be admitted that Masonic ritualists have put them in the right place.